GOD'S BIG DESIGN

Life as He intends it to be

Vaughan Roberts

IVP Books

An imprint of InterVarsity Press
Downers Grove, Illinois

InterVarsity Press
P.O. Box 1400, Downers Grove, IL 60515-1426
Internet: www.ivpress.com
E-mail: mail@ivpress.com

InterVarsity Press® is the book-publishing division of InterVarsity Christian Fellowship/USA®, a student movement active on campus at hundreds of universities, colleges and schools of nursing in the United States of America, and a member movement of the International Fellowship of Evangelical Students. For information about local and regional activities, write Public Relations Dept., InterVarsity Christian Fellowship/USA, 6400 Schroeder Rd., P.O. Box 7895, Madison, WI 53707-7895, or visit the IVCF website at <www.intervarsity.org>.

ISBN-10: 0-8308-3343-9
ISBN-13: 978-0-8308-3343-6

Printed in the United States of America ∞

Library of Congress Cataloging-in-Publication Data

Roberts, Vaughan.
  God's big design: life as He intends it to be / Vaughan Roberts.
     p. cm
  Includes bibliographical references.
  ISBN 0-8308-3343-9 (pbk.: alk. paper)
  1. Christian life—Biblical teaching. 2. Teleology. I. Title.
  BV4501.3.R637 2005
  248.4—dc22

                                                                    2005021339

P	17	16	15	14	13	12	11	10	9	8	7	6	5	4	3	2	1
Y	19	18	17	16	15	14	13	12	11	10	09	08	07	06			

To David, Ian and Vernon

"partners in the gospel from the first day"

CONTENTS

ACKNOWLEDGMENTS

I am grateful to Julian Bidgood, Dan Brockington, Annabel Heywood, Matthew Mason, Joe Martin, Glenn B. Nesbitt and Steve Tuck for commenting on the manuscript, and to Matthew Morgan for his typing.

INTRODUCTION

Some experts have been examining a letter. They take turns presenting their research: the chemist details the basic chemicals of which it consists; the physicist outlines the electrons, protons and quarks which form the basic building blocks of the paper and ink; the mathematician concludes by speaking of the fundamental equations that govern the movement of the electrons. The listeners know a great deal about the letter at the end of these presentations, but they still have no answer to some important questions: who wrote it and why? Their curiosity is only finally satisfied when Matt stands up and announces that he wrote it to his girlfriend, Ruth, to ask her to marry him.

Science can explain much about the world we live in, but it does not have all the answers. It can tell us how things work but it cannot give us an ultimate answer to the great question of meaning: why are we here? Nor can it give answers to questions of morality: how should we behave? But the Christian

FOUR BUILDING BLOCKS TO A CHRISTIAN WORLDVIEW

Creation   God made everything.

Fall   The rebellion of human beings against God has marred his perfect creation.

Redemption   God in his love has begun to fulfill his plan to restore all things through his Son Jesus.

New Creation   God's plan of salvation will be completely fulfilled when Jesus returns to introduce the new creation.

conviction is that where science is silent, God the Creator has spoken, giving us answers that we could never find by mere observation and experiment.

There are four building blocks to a Christian worldview: creation, fall, redemption and new creation.[1] In my previous two books (*God's Big Picture* and *Life's Big Questions*[2]) I have followed the Bible's story line from Genesis to Revelation as it has described each in turn. In *God's Big Design* I plan to focus on the first building block, creation, and on only two chapters of the Bible, Genesis 1—2. They provide the essential foundation for any Christian understanding of the world and our place as human beings within it.

We will be considering what Genesis 1—2 teaches about the Creator and his design for humanity, the earth, sex and marriage, and work. But even if our focus is on the very beginning of the Bible, our attention is bound to be directed often toward its end. The Creator is also the Redeemer. His original design has been spoiled by human sin but will one day be fully renewed in Christ. Genesis 1—2 provides the blueprint not just for life in this present world but also for life in the world to come—God's new creation.

You will be disappointed if you look to this book for answers to your questions about how Genesis 1—2 relates to modern science. Such discussions have their place, but there is a danger that they distract us from the Bible's message. Gordon Wenham, author of an excellent commentary on Genesis, writes:

> The Bible-versus-science debate has, most regrettably, sidetracked readers of Genesis 1. Instead of reading the chapter as a triumphant affirmation of the power and wisdom of God and the wonder of his creation, we have been too often bogged down in attempting to squeeze scripture into the mold of the latest scientific hypothesis or distorting scientific facts to fit a particular interpretation. When allowed to speak for itself, Genesis 1 looks beyond such minutiae. Its proclamation of the God of grace and power who undergirds the world and gives it purpose justifies the scientific approach to nature. Genesis 1, by further affirming the unique status of man, his place in the divine programme, and God's care for him, gives a hope to mankind that atheistic philosophies can never legitimately supply.[3]

It is hardly surprising that Genesis, coming from a prescientific age, does not address many of the questions we bring to it. However, as we study these ancient chapters we will find they offer many searching questions of their own and provide answers which are as relevant and challenging today as when they were first written.

THE DIVINE CREATOR

After their return from college, three young men were asked by their father what they had learned about God. The first spoke learnedly for 45 minutes, and the second for 20 minutes, while the youngest boy said nothing at all. But it was he who earned his father's praise: "You are the wise one; we can know nothing about God."

That is not strictly true. The Bible says that we can discover something about God from what theologians call his "general revelation" in creation (Psalm 19:1-4; Romans 1:19-20). But such knowledge is very limited. God is infinitely greater than us, so we will never be able to discover the truth about him by using our minds. But wonderfully, God has not left us in the dark. He has spoken, and in his Word, the Bible, we can discover what he is like.

God's revelation begins in Genesis 1 with the account of his creation. Genesis 1 is, above all, about God. He dominates the chapter, almost always appearing as the subject. He is the great initiator. We will notice three truths about him, each of which clashes directly with ways in which many people think today.

GOD ALONE IS ETERNAL: *Materialism Is Wrong*

The Bible opens with the famous words "In the beginning God" (Genesis 1:1). Before anything else existed, God was and had always been. The apostle John begins his Gospel with what appears to be a deliberate echo of Genesis: "In the beginning was the Word, and the Word was with God, and the Word was God. He was with God in the beginning" (John 1:1-2). From eternity there has been plurality in the Godhead. God and his Word, his Son, have always existed together. The Spirit has always existed too. He is also described as being active in the work of creation: "The Spirit of God was hovering over the waters" (Genesis 1:2). So God the Holy Trinity—Father, Son and Holy Spirit—has always existed. That quality of eternity is true of no one and nothing else.

It follows, therefore, that the philosophical concept of *materialism* is wrong. Materialism is a way of thinking that asserts the eternal existence of matter and the nonexistence of everything else. The cosmologist Carl Sagan opened his television series *Cosmos* with the claim, "The cosmos is all there is or ever was, or ever will be."[1] That is the voice of materialism: "There is no God, no spiritual realm; just matter."

Materialism is a philosophy with profound practical implications. If you believe that material things are the only reality, you are bound to live entirely for them. Materialism drives the consumerism of our culture, encapsulated by two banners above the main entrance of a London store: "I shop therefore I am" and "Buy me, I'll change your life."

Of course the slogans can never deliver all they offer. Materialism has no satisfying response to the reality of death. So, as the expression goes, "We spend our youth attaining wealth, and our wealth attaining youth."[2] But the Bible insists that materialism is wrong. God alone is the ultimate reality; he alone is eternal.

GOD ALONE IS CREATOR: *Accidentalism Is Wrong*

Genesis 1 asserts that God created everything: "In the beginning God created the heavens and the earth." At first, after his initial creation of the heavens and the earth, "the earth was formless and empty." It had no shape and no inhabitants (Genesis 1:1-2). God proceeds to put this right, in the six creative days, by forming and filling the earth.

Genesis 1 is a carefully structured literary account. On the first three days God forms the universe. He then fills it on the second three days. There is a parallel between days 1 and 4, 2 and 5, and 3 and 6.

Table 1.1. The Six Days of Creation

Forming		Filling	
Day 1	Light	Day 4	Sun, moon and stars
Day 2	Sea and sky	Day 5	Sea creatures and birds
Day 3	Land and vegetation	Day 6	Land-based creatures and humans

On the first day God creates light and then separates the light from the darkness (Genesis 1:3-5). On the fourth day he creates lights, the sun and moon, for the day and the night, and then adds, in a great throwaway line, "he also made the stars" (Genesis 1:14-19, esp. verse 16). A fraction of those stars are visible to the naked eye. It has been suggested that if

IS THERE A CONFLICT BETWEEN SCIENCE AND GENESIS 1—2?

The difficulties between science and the biblical account of creation are significantly reduced once we understand the limitations of science and the nature of the Bible.

1. The Limitations of Science

"Fact" and theory. The scientific method has advanced our understanding and enabled progress in countless ways. However, the knowledge science produces should not be exaggerated.

Science progresses by producing theories on the basis of experiment and observation. Much that is presented as fact, not least in the area of origins and evolution, is still only a theory and is disputed even within the scientific community.

"How?" "why?" and "who?" questions. Science is limited to the "how" question: "How does the world work?" It has nothing to say in answer to the "why" and "who" questions: "Why are we here?" and "Who made us?" These are addressed by the Bible. In general, science and the Bible are complementary, not contradictory.

the total number of stars were to be divided among the world's present population, each individual would receive two trillion of them[3]—and God made every one.

On the second day God creates the sea and the sky (Genesis 1:6-8); on the fifth day he creates sea creatures and birds to live in the water and the air (Genesis 1:20-23). There are currently

2. The nature of the Bible

Divine and human. The Bible is God's Word, but he chose to use humans to write it, "as they were carried along by the Holy Spirit" (2 Peter 1:21). Those humans wrote in many different literary genres including prophecy, poetry, history, law and apocalyptic. If we are to understand any part of the Bible correctly, we must appreciate what sort of writing it is. For example, the description of God "pitching a tent for the sun" (Psalm 19:4) is clearly poetic and should not be taken literally. Christian opinions differ as to exactly how we should read Genesis 1—2, even among those who have a high view of Scripture as the Word of God. Some argue that there are clues within the text which suggest that we are not meant to view it as a literal, chronological account. To take just one example, the word *day* appears in the Hebrew of Genesis 2:4 when it clearly does not refer to a twenty-four hour period but rather to the longer time of God's whole creative work. That suggests that *day* may refer to a longer period in Genesis 1 as well.

See the "Further Reading" section on page 119 for some recommended books if you want to pursue this subject further.

JESUS AND CREATION

Jesus Christ is fully divine. Along with the Father and the Holy Spirit, he is transcendent and distinct from the created order.

Jesus Christ Precedes All Things

- "In the beginning was the Word, and the Word was with God, and the Word was God. He was with God in the beginning." (John 1:1-2)

- "He is before all things." (Colossians 1:17)

Jesus Christ Creates All Things

- "Through him all things were made; without him nothing was made that has been made." (John 1:3)

- "For by him all things were created: things in heaven and on earth, visible and invisible, whether thrones or powers or rulers or authorities; all things were created by him and for him." (Colossians 1:16)

- "Through [his Son] he made the universe." (Hebrews 1:2)

Jesus Christ Sustains All Things

- "In him all things hold together." (Colossians 1:17)

Jesus Christ Rules All Things

- "He is the image of the invisible God, the firstborn* over all creation." (Colossians 1:15)

- "He appointed [his Son] heir of all things." (Hebrews 1:2)

---

*The word *firstborn* does not imply that Jesus Christ is the first created being. That would deny the clear teaching of the Bible that he is eternal (John 1:1-2). *Firstborn* speaks not of Christ's origins but of his position. The firstborn son in the biblical world was the leader of the next generation. Christ, as the uncreated Creator of everything, has authority over all he has made.

about thirty-five thousand known species of fish; every year another hundred are discovered. And God made them all.

On day three God creates a fertile earth (Genesis 1:9-13), and on day six he creates animals to live on the land and human beings in his image (Genesis 1:24-27).

It is a comprehensive account of creation: everything is included. The apostle Paul centuries later writes these extraordinary words about Jesus Christ, his Father's agent in creation: "By him *all things* were created: things in heaven and on earth, visible and invisible, whether thrones or powers or rulers or authorities; *all things* were created by him and for him." And just as Christ made everything, so he sustains everything. Every breath we take is only by divine permission: "In him *all things* hold together" (Colossians 1:16-17, emphasis added).

God alone is Creator, and so it follows that "accidentalism"[4] is wrong. Accidentalism is the view that everything in this world is the result of no Creator, no guiding hand, but rather chance alone. The Big Bang, it is believed, was purely accidental. Likewise, the process of natural selection which, it is claimed, has produced the current multiple forms of life on earth is under no one's control. In the words of Richard Dawkins, professor of the public understanding of science at Oxford University: "If [natural selection] can be said to play the role of watchmaker in nature, it is the blind watchmaker."[5] But can we really believe that all that exists is the result of a series of accidents?

Isaac Newton built a model of the solar system to help him

in his studies. An atheistic friend asked him who had made it. Newton said, "No one."

His friend responded, "Don't be ridiculous! A structure as intricate as that must have been made by someone."

Newton, who was a convinced theist, then made his point: "If it is obvious to you that this model needed a maker, why don't you come to the same conclusion when confronted with the real universe?"[6]

The "argument from design" has often been dismissed over the years, but it is still powerful. Think of the vastness of the universe. The nearest star clusters in our galaxy are 170,000 light-years away. Another thirty galaxies complete what astronomers refer to as the "local group"—even though one of them, the Andromeda Spiral, is some 2.2 million light-years away. No wonder Douglas Adams could write in his *Hitchhiker's Guide to the Galaxy*: "Space is big. Really big. You won't believe how vastly mind-boggling big it is. I mean you may think it is a long way down the road to the Chemist, but that's just peanuts to space."[7]

God's creation is not only vast; it also consists of amazing details. "The tiniest cell constitutes an automated factory of unimagined functional complexity. . . . The DNA code contained within a cell carries as much information as a library."[8] Darwin himself once wrote: "When I think of the eye I become feverish."[9] Can it really be explained satisfactorily by natural selection alone?

There is very good evidence for "microevolution" within species. "Macroevolution," as an explanation of the origin of all living things from nonliving substance, is a theory that continues to be questioned by many. But even if you broadly accept its account of how the world came to be as it is, can you believe that it just happened by chance?

The fundamental choice is not between creation and evolution, but between creation and accident. The Bible insists that God alone is Creator; he made everything.

GOD ALONE IS SOVEREIGN: *Humanism Is Wrong*

God's awesome power is evident in Genesis 1. He just speaks and the universe comes into existence. "God said, 'Let there be light,' and there was light" (Genesis 1:3): from creation to cosmos in just four words. The refrain "God said, 'Let there be,'" or some close equivalent appears at the beginning of each creative day. And in all but the first and fourth days they are followed by the words: "and it was so."

You can tell how powerful someone is by the effect of their words. The inexperienced teacher says "Quiet" to the class repeatedly, with little effect. But if the experienced teacher says it, there is an instant hush. And so, when God speaks, things happen. He is all-powerful. He speaks and the whole creation comes into being:

> By the word of the LORD were the heavens made,
>   their starry host by the breath of his mouth.
> (Psalm 33:6)

As the mighty Creator of everything, God has authority over everything. He alone is sovereign, and so humanism is wrong.

Humanism is a way of thinking that places humanity at the center of the universe. There is no God; he is simply the product of our minds and imaginations. We created him, not the other way round. So, we are the masters of our fate. It is up to us to decide how we will live. In the words of the poet Charles Swinburne: "Glory to man in the highest! For man is the master of things."[10]

The teaching of Genesis will not allow such arrogance. God alone is sovereign. He is the rightful owner of all that he has made, including us:

> For the LORD is the great God,
>   the great King above all gods.
> In his hand are the depths of the earth,
>   and the mountain peaks belong to him.
> The sea is his, for he made it,
>   and his hands formed the dry land.
> Come, let us bow down in worship,
>   let us kneel before the LORD our Maker;
> for he is our God
>   and we are the people of his pasture,
>   the flock under his care. (Psalm 95:3-7)

God is transcendent, above and beyond all that he has made, and over it too. We are not the masters of the world; God is.

MEANING

The fact that God is Creator has many consequences for how we think about and live in the world. I will focus on the im-

THE DIVINE CREATOR

1. God alone is eternal   →   Materialism is wrong

2. God alone is Creator   →   Accidentalism is wrong

3. God alone is sovereign →   Humanism is wrong

plications in three areas: meaning, morality and worship.
The philosopher Bertrand Russell once asserted that

> the beliefs that man is the product of causes which had
> no provision of the end they were achieving; that his or-
> igin, his growth, his hopes, his fears, his loves and beliefs
> are but the outcome of accidental collations of atoms . . .
> that all the labours of the ages . . . are destined to extinc-
> tion in the vast death of the solar system   if not quite
> beyond dispute, are yet so nearly certain, that no philos
> ophy which rejects them can hope to stand. Only within
> the scaffolding of these truths, only on the firm founda-
> tion of unyielding despair, can the soul's habitation
> henceforth be safely built.[11]

Those words are depressing and yet entirely logical. If there
is no Creator, there is no meaning. In the words of Francis
Bacon, "Man now realises that he's an accident, that he is a
completely futile being, and that he has to play out the game
without reason."[12] It is no surprise that as belief in a Creator
God has declined, a sense of despair has increased. A lost,

largely joyless generation is where accidentalism leads.

I can see why some convince themselves that they must accept that view, but I cannot understand why someone would happily choose it. It is a philosophy of despair: "Life has no reasons; a struggling through the gloom and the senseless end of it is the insult of the tomb."[13]

It is very different for those who believe in a Creator God. Life makes sense. We know where we come from and where we are heading. The Bible teaches us that God made everything, in the first place, and one day he will bring everything to completion when Christ returns. That past and future makes sense of the present. We live in God's world, and our purpose is to live his way for his glory in relationship to him, the one who made us in his image. God describes human beings as those "whom I created for my glory" (Isaiah 43:7). We are not here on earth to make our own name, to establish our own little empire or to please ourselves. We are rather to long that God's name be hallowed, his kingdom come and his will be done. It is in relationship to our Creator that we find our place in his world.

MORALITY

If we are just accidents and there is no God, then there can be no fixed morality. Right and wrong become purely subjective concepts which we create for ourselves rather than given realities that derive from the nature of our Creator. The French existentialist Jean-Paul Sartre was very honest on this point: "It is extremely embarrassing that God does not exist, for there disappears with him all possibility of finding values in an intelligible heaven. . . . We find no values or demands to turn to."[14]

It is often said that religion is the cause of much of the evil in the world. It is undoubtedly true that many terrible things have been done in the name of God. People have abused Christian teaching to serve their own interests. But we must not forget that some of the worst terrors of the twentieth century were committed by atheists such as Adolf Hitler, Joseph Stalin, Mao Tse Tung and Pol Pot. Surely that cannot be a coincidence. Without fixed values there is little moral constraint.

In a review of Jonathan Glover's book *Humanity: A Moral History of the Twentieth Century*, Bryan Appleyard commented.

"God died in the nineteenth century and Nietzsche danced on his grave. The foundation of the external moral law was destroyed and, in its place, was a vacuum, soon gleefully filled by the narcotics of Nazism and Communism. It may not be possible to say that the death of God led directly to the death ovens; but equally, nobody can ignore the fact that the cruellest era in history was also the first to deny the existence of an external moral force." The question the book poses is how, without such a moral law, "can we stop the long nightmare of the twentieth century from spilling over into the twenty-first?"[15]

That question remains unanswered. Of course, individual atheists can be moral, but their morality is an entirely relative concept. For Ernest Hemingway, "what is moral is what you feel good after, and what is immoral is what you feel bad after."[16] But what feels good to one person feels bad to another. Others try to define morality by looking for the effects of an action on others. According to one popular view, utilitarianism, the right action is that which aims for the greatest good of the greatest number. But what if someone argues that, for the good of the majority, the handicapped, the elderly and even a whole race should be disposed of? Most atheists would be horrified by that argument. They may insist that eugenics, euthanasia and genocide are wicked, but on what basis? That is just their view: right and wrong, good and evil exist only in the eye of the beholder. If morality is just personal choice, how can it be enforced?

By contrast, if God made the world, then right and wrong are not merely social constructs. Good and evil are fixed realities which derive from his eternal character. The tree of the knowledge of good and evil was not planted by Adam and Eve. God placed it in the middle of Eden at the very beginning. It stands as a powerful symbol of the eternal, unchanging standards of the Creator which we are commanded to obey. Even if we do not enforce them, he will on the Day of Judgment.

WORSHIP

As those who have been made by God, we belong to him. The only right response is to acknowledge him as Lord and worship him. The twenty-four elders in John's vision lay their crowns before God's throne and say,

You are worthy, our Lord and God,
    to receive glory and honor and power,
for you created all things,
    and by your will they were created
    and have their being. (Revelation 4:11)

We all need to worship something. If we turn from the one true God who made us, we will fill the vacuum with some other god to live for and adore. In Paul's words, we worship and serve "created things rather than the Creator" (Romans 1:25). It could be our career, money, possessions, some other person or an object in a temple. The Bible calls all such worship "idolatry." We should not live for ourselves or anything in this world. There is only one God, and he alone demands our worship: the Father, Son and Holy Spirit who created us.

From the very beginning we have failed to worship God as we should. Adam and Eve were not to eat from the tree of the knowledge of good and evil (Genesis 2:17). They disobeyed, and human beings have followed in their footsteps ever since. Instead of seeking to live by God's standards in relationship with him, we choose to go our own way. We have made a mess of our lives and God's Word as a result.

And yet, despite our disobedience, God has chosen not to turn away from creation but to redeem it. God the Holy Trinity alone created everything and has the power to re-create. Just as the Father brought the first creation into being through the agency of his Son by his word, so his new creation is made possible by the work of Christ and the word of the Spirit through the gospel.

● BIBLE STUDY: ACTS 17:16-34

What are the equivalents in our society to the idols in Athens (v. 16)?

What can we learn from

- Paul's reaction and response to the idols he saw (vv. 16-18)?
- Paul's introduction to his address (vv. 22-23)?

Why do you think Paul starts his presentation of the truth by speaking of God as Creator (v. 24)?

What do we learn about the Creator God from verses 24-29?

- How does this thinking clash with the world's thinking?
- How does it challenge our thinking as Christians? our behavior as Christians?

Why is it so important that we repent (vv. 30-31)?

How are the responses of the Athenians mirrored today (vv. 32-34)?

How will you respond to what you have learned

- in this passage?
- in the chapter you've just read?

GOD'S DESIGN FOR HUMANITY

Two items appeared side by side in a museum. One was a skeleton of a Roman slave whose body had been left at the bottom of a well. In life he had no freedom or rights, and in death he had been disposed of like a piece of rubbish. The other exhibit was a Roman altar dedicated to "the divine Emperor Augustus."[1] The contrast between the two could not be greater. Both represent a false understanding of who we are as human beings.

What does it mean to be a human being? That is a crucial question for each of us individually. The answer will give us a sense of personal identity and a knowledge of how we should live. It is also a vitally important question for the whole of society. It takes us right to the front line of many of the political and ethical battles raging in our culture today. What do we think about abortion, euthanasia and stem cell research? And, more broadly, what education, housing, penal or economic policy should we adopt? Our answers to those questions will be greatly influenced, and in some cases determined, by our understanding of who we are as human beings.

Genesis 1—2 teaches two fundamental truths about us, each of which challenges the false views represented by the museum exhibits. We are created by God and should therefore submit to him. No human being should ever be worshiped. But we are also made in the image of God and therefore have great dignity. No human being should ever be counted worthless.

CREATED BY GOD

We are created beings. In the Darwinian view, all that exists is the product of "the impersonal plus time plus chance."[2] The Bible disagrees. We are created beings, not accidents.

There are two complementary accounts of creation in Genesis 1—2. Genesis 1, structured in six days, presents the creation of humanity as the great creative climax. Genesis 2 looks at the same events from a different angle and with a different focus. This time human beings are not so much the pinnacle of the story as the pivot. Genesis 1 places humanity in our cosmic setting. Genesis 2 then shows us to be absolutely central. The creation of man and woman is described again, but in more detail than in Genesis 1:26-27:

> The LORD God formed the man from the dust of the ground and breathed into his nostrils the breath of life, and the man became a living being. (Genesis 2:7)

So the LORD God caused the man to fall into a deep sleep;
and while he was sleeping, he took one of the man's ribs
and closed up the place with flesh. Then the LORD God
made a woman from the rib he had taken out of the man,
and he brought her to the man. (Genesis 2:21-22)

There is room for discussion about exactly how we read
these verses. Some take Genesis 2 literally: what was dust one
minute became a man the next; when God created woman he
really did take one of Adam's ribs and formed her out of it.
Others believe the writer is using symbolic language. They accept that there could have been apelike forebears to human
beings; then, at some point in time, God breathed his life into
two individuals who became the first Homo sapiens made in
God's image. Wherever we stand on these issues, the crucial
point is that human beings were created by God.

Professor Edmund Leach, former provost of King's College,
Cambridge, once argued that human beings "have become
like gods. Isn't it about time we understood our divinity? Science offers us total mastery over our environment."[3] That is a
particularly brazen expression of an attitude shared by many:
"We are the masters of the world, not God." Too often, if we
acknowledge God's existence at all, it is on our terms. We decide what type of god we want and then mold him to suit our
tastes. And we restrict him to certain places: the "spiritual"
realm and religious buildings. We try to keep him out of the
rest of life. We can even feel as though we are doing him a favor if we turn up in church.

What folly! Paul's words to the Athenians rebuke us: "The God who made the world and everything in it is the Lord of heaven and earth and does not live in temples built by hands. And he is not served by human hands, as if he needed anything, because he himself gives all men life and breath and everything else" (Acts 17:24). The prophet Isaiah had the right attitude:

We are the clay, you are the potter;
we are all the work of your hand. (Isaiah 64:8)

We dare not boast about our possessions, physique, abilities, or achievements; they are all undeserved gifts of God's grace. We are dependent on him, not he on us. We should heed the words of the psalmist: "Know that the LORD is God. / It is he who has made us, and we are his" (Psalm 100:3). We belong to him and we should live for him.

We are physical beings. "The LORD God formed the man from the dust of the ground" (Genesis 2:7). He made us out of matter, so we are material beings. God is not just concerned with our spirits; he made our bodies too.

In some religions and philosophies, material and physical things are degraded. They are seen as a lesser order of reality, or even an illusion, from which we should seek to escape. Salvation is understood as the release of the soul from the prison of the physical body and the material world. But the Bible never speaks in those terms. Our bodies are important because God made them.

It is no coincidence that Christians have taken the lead in establishing hospitals wherever they have gone throughout the world. God made us physical beings, and he cares about our physical health. He also cares about how we use our bodies. That is why Paul can say: "Offer your bodies as living sacrifices, holy and pleasing to God" (Romans 12:1). God is not just concerned with our spirits: how we think and feel. He also cares about where we go with our feet, what we look at with our eyes, and how we use our tongues, our sexual organs and our hands.

We are sexual beings. "So God created man in his own image, in the image of God he created him; male and female he created them" (Genesis 1:27).

A friend recently showed me a fascinating article from the student newspaper of the University of Chicago.[4] It reported a meeting, jointly sponsored by the University's Feminist Majority, Queers and Associates, and the Center for Gender Studies, to discuss the need for gender-neutral toilets on campus. The convenor of the event stated that the toilets will be called "gender-neutral," because "co-ed"

is generally used to refer to two sexes while the gender-neutral tends to be associated with more diversity and fluidity within the sex-gender continuum. As our aim is to make everyone, no matter what their gender and/or sexual persona is, more comfortable, we are using the term gender-neutral.

The idea was supported by one student interviewed on campus: "I believe that if all parts of the body were treated equally, and there was not so much emphasis on genitalia, then people could move beyond gender differences and grow mentally and socially."

That discussion reflects a trend within Western society to diminish the significance of gender difference. We are encouraged to see ourselves not so much as men and women but simply as human beings. Simone de Beauvoir, one of the founders of the modern feminist movement, once said, "One is not born, but rather becomes a woman."[5] She is arguing that, apart from the obvious biological ones, the differences between men and women are imposed by society. It is undoubtedly true that culture and nurture do play an important role, but as the Bible insists, so do creation and nature. We must resist any attempt to use gender differences as an excuse for sexism. God certainly made men and woman equal, both created in his image. Yet he also made us different; he designed us to complement each other. It is that difference which is reflected in the New Testament's teaching that in the family and the church men should take the ultimate lead. It is striking that the apostle Paul bases his teaching in this area not on culture, which changes with time, but on God's design in creation (1 Corinthians 11:8; 1 Timothy 2:13).

Society's confusion about gender is also evident in Great Britain's 2004 Gender Recognition Act. The legislation arose out of a psychological condition known as gender dysphoria.

This is not to be confused with intersex conditions, where there is a biological abnormality. Those who suffer from dysphoria are biologically normal, but psychologically feel that they are trapped in the wrong body. So, for example, someone might be physically a male but feel, psychologically, female. Such people should receive our sympathy and support. We cannot imagine how difficult it must be to cope in these circumstances. Some have had these feelings for as long as they can remember. But Christians cannot agree that those who suffer in this way should be allowed to undergo a "sex change" operation. Each year about ninety such operations are performed in the National Health Service. The Recognition Act gives these "transsexuals" the right to obtain a new birth certificate. So, for example, a man can get a certificate stating he was born a woman and can then legally marry another man.

The thinking that has led to this act gives greater weight to the mind than the body. How I view myself psychologically is seen as more important than what my body declares me to be. But our gender is not just a veneer that can be changed at will. It is fundamental to who God has made us to be. We are not simply human beings; we are male and female: sexual beings.

HUMANITY: CREATED BY GOD

- Created beings
- Physical beings
- Sexual beings

IN THE IMAGE OF GOD

We are not just animals. Peter Singer, professor of bioethics at Princeton University, has coined a new term: *speciesism,* "a prejudice or attitude in favour of the interests of one's own species against those of members of other species."[6] He argues that all sentient creatures, with the ability to experience pleasure or pain, should be granted the same rights as human beings. There is no excuse for any discrimination, for "all animals are equal."[7]

Elsewhere Singer defines a person as a "self-conscious or rational being" who is therefore able to make decisions.[8] It follows that some primates are persons according to Singer's definition, but some humans, such as a newborn baby or an elderly person suffering from advanced Alzheimer's disease, are not. It is not surprising that Singer supports euthanasia, abortion on demand and even, in certain circumstances, infanticide. He argues that parents should have the right to have their unhealthy babies killed in the first twenty-eight days of life. That allows them time to decide whether it is better "not to continue with the life that has begun very badly."[9] What is to stop such an action if the baby is not a person?

Do you see how crucially important our subject is? So much follows from our understanding of what a human being is.

Materialists argue that there is nothing more to us than the atoms and molecules of which we are made. We have no soul or spirit. Francis Crick, who discovered the double-helix structure of DNA, once said, "You, your joys and sorrows, your memories and ambitions, your sense of personal identity and free will, are in fact no more than the behaviour of a vast assembly of nerve cells and their associated molecules."[10] We are, says Richard Dawkins, "survival machines—robot vehicles blindly programmed to preserve the selfish molecules known as genes."[11] There is, therefore, no difference in essence between us and animals. If that is the case, why not simply "put down" those who are unwanted at birth, become lame or are no longer useful in old age? We do that with animals; why not with humans?

The materialist position is a typical example of what Christian neuroscientist Donald MacKay called "nothing buttery," the belief that we are "nothing but" the material of which we consist.[12] But that does not follow. Yes, we are physical, material beings. In that sense we are animals. But that is not all. All humans, born or unborn, fit or healthy, conscious or unconscious, are not merely "persons" but spiritual beings, made in the image of God.

The image of God. "Then God said, 'Let us make man in our image, in our likeness, and let them rule over the fish of the sea and the birds of the air, over the livestock, over all the earth, and over all the creatures that move along the ground.' So God created man in his own image, in the image of God he created him, male and female he created them" (Genesis 1:26-27).

We are not gods but we are like God. The words *image* and *likeness* both speak of similarity. We are designed to reflect God in a way that no other creature was. Theologians have spent centuries discussing what it means for us to be made in God's image. They tend to focus on three themes, although different scholars have given different weight to each.

THE IMAGE OF GOD

- We reflect God

- We represent God

- We can relate to God

WE REFLECT GOD

Many theologians have started by stressing that we are like God. In some senses at least, we are reflections of him. For example:

- *We are rational (capable of reflective thought).* God can say to humans what he could never say to animals: "Come now, let us reason together" (Isaiah 1:18). God is a speaking God. We too are able to speak and understand.

- *We are moral (responsible for the choices we make).* Our consciences tell us the difference between right and wrong. As Paul writes: "The requirements of the law are written on [our] hearts" (Romans 2:15).

- *We are social (able to love).* God's very nature is love: from eternity there has been a relationship of mutual love within the three persons of the Godhead. We most reflect God when we love as he loves. "God is love. Who-

ever lives in love lives in God, and God in him" (1 John
4:16).

- *We are artistic (able to be creative).* God alone is the Creator, but as those made in his image, we too are able to
be creative, producing music, art and architecture (Genesis 4:21; 1 Chronicles 2:7).

- *We are spiritual (drawn to worship).* We were designed by
God with an awareness of the transcendent and a capacity to "seek him and perhaps reach out for him and find
him" (Acts 17:27).[13]

These are undoubtedly significant ways in which we reflect
God. But we should be wary of locating the image of God in
any of these particular qualities. Some of them can be seen, at
least in part, in the animal kingdom too. The Bible never spells
out exactly how we are like God, it just states the fact that we
are. This is surely one of the reasons why he has forbidden us
from making images of him. God has already created an image
of himself: human beings.

WE REPRESENT GOD

The emphasis of Genesis 1 is that, as the image of God, we human beings are his representatives. Both references to our creation in God's image are followed by commands to rule over
everything else he has made:

Then God said, "Let us make man in our image, in our
likeness, and let them rule over the fish of the sea and the

birds of the air, over the livestock, over all the earth, and over all the creatures that move along the ground."

So God created man in his own image, in the image of God he created him; male and female he created them.

God blessed them and said to them, "Be fruitful and increase in number; fill the earth and subdue it. Rule over the fish of the sea and the birds of the air and over every living creature that moves on the ground." (Genesis 1:26-28)

A friend of mine was appointed to represent his company in another country. He had authority, but within limits. It was his responsibility to carry out the policies that had been decided by the board of directors at the head office. We humans are God's representatives on earth. We have been set apart from the rest of the created order and established as his appointed rulers over it. We will think more about what that means in practice in the next chapter.

WE CAN RELATE TO GOD

After creating the first humans, God speaks to them in verse 28, giving them their instructions. He never speaks to the animals, birds or fish. There would be no point: they would not understand and could not respond because they had not been created with that capacity. But, as those uniquely made in his image, we human beings have been designed to live in relationship with our Creator.

John Calvin wrote, "All men are born to live to the end that they may know God."[14] That relationship is fundamental to what it means to be human. Many people simply function with their eyes on the earth, trying to find a partner, establish a home and then provide for themselves and their families. Propagation and material provision are certainly important, but if they are all that matter to us, then we are living as if we are no different from the animals. We have been created for much more than that.

We should not simply look down to this world, we should also look up to God. "Man's basic relationship is upward rather than downward or horizontal. He is created to relate to God in a way that none of the other created beings are."[15] That truth should be reflected in our own goals for life and use of time and in our education and training of others. Are we content in schools and at home simply to prepare the next generation to be economically useful? If so, we are treating them as little more than animals, mere units of production. Above all, we should be concerned to raise them as those who know their God.

"GOD DON'T MAKE NO JUNK"

All sorts of consequences flow from the glorious truth that we have been made in God's image. For a start, it should influence our attitude toward ourselves.

Perhaps you are someone who suffers from low self-esteem. It may be that others have looked down on you in the family, at college or at work, and you have been made to feel worthless. If so, remember that you have been made in God's image.

An African American in the 1960s was bowed down by racial abuse. But then a friend reminded him, "you've been made by God, and God don't make no junk." Every time he suffered from the demeaning words or attitudes of others, he repeated those words to himself: "God don't make no junk." He was gradually able to lift his head up high again. Let us allow the same truth to encourage us when others seek to put us down. As those who have been created in God's image, we have great dignity.

"YOU SHALL NOT MURDER"

The dignity of human beings in the image of God should affect not just our understanding of ourselves but our treatment of others. After the flood God told Noah,

> Whoever sheds the blood of man,
>   by man shall his blood be shed;
> for in the image of God
>   has God made man. (Genesis 9:6)

Murder is absolutely forbidden: to kill the image is to do violence to God himself. The destruction of human life must never be viewed lightly. And yet increasingly abortion and even euthanasia are seen as just medical operations, with little or no moral significance.

In some parts of the world many parents choose abortion when they learn that a fetus is female. In China 120 male ba-

bies are born for every 100 females. In some Indian villages
the figure is nearer 150.

> Social scientists say that India is missing forty million
> girls, aborted en masse over the years by parents, rich
> and poor, who saw them as a liability, while boys are
> cherished for continuing the family line and providing
> economic security. All over India, since the 1980's
> when the country was flooded with cheap ultra-sound
> technology, this mobile killing machine   has been
> doing its lethal work. . . . In some villages no girls have
> been born for years. The Indian Medical Association es-
> timates that five million female foetuses are aborted
> each year.[16]

In Great Britain, abortion was illegal for centuries except
when it was performed with the intention of saving the
mother's life. The position changed with the 1967 Abortion
Act, which allowed for abortion in certain limited circumstances in the first twenty-eight weeks of pregnancy (reduced
to twenty-four weeks in 1990). The abortion rate rose dramat-
ically, finally settling at about 180,000 every year. Great Britain now has abortion effectively on demand up to twenty-four
weeks, and children are aborted for even minor handicaps after that. In one recent notorious case a late term pregnancy
was terminated when it was discovered that the fetus had a
cleft pallet, even though the law allows termination only for
major handicaps at such a late stage. Within a lifetime Great

Britain has seen a rapid slide from abortion for serious health reasons or rape to abortion on demand; from abortion for significant impairment to abortion for any fetal abnormality; from abortion for medical reasons to abortion for social reasons (it's just not convenient to have the baby).

I am well aware that this is sensitive ground. All sorts of factors lead to abortions, and many are undertaken very reluctantly and after serious thought. We should be wary of glib condemnation, and we must stress God's grace and mercy offered to all. Abortion is not an unforgivable sin. But we must also acknowledge that the destruction of so many babies, made in God's image, is an evil which brings shame on us all.

Who can say that infanticide will not come next? In a recent radio program Ellie Lee, coordinator of the British Pro-Choice Forum, said, "A woman should not only be allowed to abort a foetus for any reason right up until the moment of birth, but also to kill a disabled child after birth."[17] That may sound inconceivable now, but euthanasia seemed unthinkable a few decades ago. Now it is frighteningly easy to imagine its introduction: it is already legal in Belgium and Holland. The aging population of Western societies will place a massive burden on a diminishing workforce. Would it not be easier if the elderly could be persuaded to take a pill now that they are no longer contributing to the wealth of society? What is to stop us if human beings are just animals? We put the pet to sleep; why not Grandpa? And if he is suffering from dementia or a terminal illness, are we not being merciful if we end his pain? But who are we to decide when a life is worth living, even our own? We have been made in God's image. Our lives belong to him, and he alone has the authority to decide when they should end.

Jesus taught that we break God's prohibition of murder not just when we literally kill someone but when we are unjustifiably angry with them (Matthew 5:22). The fact that all humans are made in God's image forbids any degrading treatment of others. We were rightly appalled by the terrible pictures of prisoner abuse in the aftermath of the 2003 invasion of Iraq. But do we recognize how easily we too descend into degrading treatment of others? There is no excuse for sexism, racism, snobbery or bullying. Every person we encounter—from king to cleaner, prime minister to prisoner and judge to janitor—demands our respect.

It is not enough simply to avoid mistreating others. Do we keep our distance from those who are different from us or do we rather make an effort to break down barriers? We are all guilty of attitudes and actions which demean others, and we must repent.

A respect for every individual should influence our personal dealings with all those we meet. It should also influence public policy. We should encourage governments to remember in their formulation of housing, penal and asylum policy that they are dealing not just with problems or statistics but with people made in the image of God.

THE TRUE IMAGE

Even after the fall of Adam and Eve, the image of God remains in human beings (Genesis 5:1-3; James 3:9). But it is corrupted. Sin has spoiled our humanity, and as God's appointed rulers over the earth, we have brought everything else down with us. If God is to restore creation, he must restore humanity so that once again we reflect him as we should, represent him properly as rulers on his behalf, and relate to him perfectly. All this has been made possible through his Son, the Lord Jesus.[18]

Jesus Christ is the perfect human being; the perfect reflection of his Father. "He is the image of the invisible God" (Colossians 1:15). "The Son is the radiance of God's glory and the exact representation of his being" (Hebrews 1:3). By his perfect life, his death in our place, and his resurrection from the dead, he makes it possible for us to be restored to true humanity. Those who have trusted in Christ are now gradually being transformed into his likeness by the Spirit (2 Corinthians 3:18). One day, in the new creation, that process will be complete. "We know that when he appears, we shall be like him, for we shall see him as he is" (1 John 3:2). "And just as we have borne the likeness of the earthly man [Adam], so shall we bear the likeness of the man from heaven [Christ]" (1 Corinthians 15:49).

● BIBLE STUDY: GENESIS 1:26-27

What does it mean to be made in God's image?

How does the Bible's understanding of humanity differ from the ways in which those around us think?

What practical effects do the different understandings have on

- how we view ourselves?
- how we treat others (see Genesis 9:5-6; Matthew 5:21-22; James 3:9-12)?

Which groups of people is our society failing to treat properly as those made in God's image?

How could the church be different?

How might we ensure that the Christian voice is heard in society?

GOD'S DESIGN FOR THE EARTH

It all happens so suddenly. One moment everyone is carrying on with their daily business quite normally, but within a few minutes everything changes forever. Tornados rip through Los Angeles, a massive snow storm pounds New Delhi, hail the size of grapefruit batters Tokyo, and in New York the temperature swings from sweltering to freezing in one day.

The Hollywood blockbuster *The Day After Tomorrow* packed cinemas around the world with its dramatic account of a cataclysmic environmental crisis. It is hard to believe it would have had such an impact twenty or even ten years ago; it would have seemed too fanciful. But now it is all too possible for many to imagine such global disasters, even if scientists tell us they could not come in quite the manner depicted by the film. One expert has written: "We are barraged by data that render questionable the survival of our culture, our species, and even our planet as a viable home for conscious life. . . .

Despair in this context is the loss of the assumption that the species will inevitably pull through."[1]

For many years now we have seen the depletion of the earth's natural resources, accelerated by population growth and rapidly increasing energy demands. Industrialization has led to pollution through chemical, biological and nuclear waste. In recent times we have become increasingly aware of the resulting damage caused to the atmosphere. By the year 2000 the hole in the ozone over the Antarctic extended over 10 million square miles.[2] Debate continues over the extent, causes and seriousness of global warming and climate change, but there is a general recognition that it is a significant prob lem with serious potential consequences. The Kyoto Protocol in 1997, with its goal of reducing greenhouse gas emissions, was an attempted response by the nations of the world. Few believe it has gone far enough or is really workable, and the American withdrawal under President Bush significantly limited its potential impact.

These concerns combine to produce great anxiety about the future. It is no exaggeration to speak of an environmental crisis. What is the Christian response? Our answer will depend on our understanding of the world in which we live. In this chapter I will focus on three fundamental truths taught in the Bible.

THE EARTH WAS CREATED BY GOD

Many believe the universe came into existence by accident. Then, according to the Darwinian view, the process of evo-

UNDERSTANDING OUR WORLD

1. The earth was created by God
2. The earth was entrusted to human beings
3. The earth will be redeemed by Christ

lution took over. There was no Creator, no guiding hand, just chance. The result is a low view of nature. If things exist simply by accident, they have no intrinsic value. If you believe in the survival of the fittest, what is to stop you from imposing your human strength on the rest of nature without regard for any of the consequences, except those that directly affect you?

Partly as a reaction to this diminished view of the natural world, a pantheistic view originating from the East has become increasingly popular in the West. Nature is regarded as divine. The whole universe is believed to be God, or part of God. It is not distinct from him but rather emanates out of him. Many have adopted James Lovelock's Gaia Theory.[3] The earth is viewed as a living, self-regulating organism. It is a unified whole in which everything is bound together: "all is one." Some add a religious element to the theory: we are bound together with everything else in the universe and with God too, because God is in everything and is everything.

The opening words of the Bible challenge both these contrasting views of the earth. One is too low and the other too high. Nature is neither an accident nor divine. Everything that exists was created by God (Genesis 1:1). He is the transcendent God, above and beyond all that he has made. In the words of C. S. Lewis, "Pantheism is a creed, not so much false as hopelessly behind the times. Once, before creation, it would have been true to say that everything was God. But God created; he caused things to be other than himself."[1] The earth is distinct from him and lower than him, but it has great value. He created a good, ordered and beautiful world.

THE WORLD GOD MADE

- *Good.* "God saw that it was good." (Genesis 1:10)

- *Ordered.* ". . . according to their various kinds." (Genesis 1:11)

- *Beautiful.* ". . . pleasing to the eye." (Genesis 2:9)

- *Glorifies God.* "The heavens declare the glory of God." (Psalm 19:1)

- *Unfinished.* "Fill the earth and subdue it." (Genesis 1:28)

CREATION IS GOOD

Many philosophies and religions, especially in the East, are dualistic: they divide the spiritual and the material. The material and physical is seen as either evil or illusory. God is believed to be concerned exclusively with the spiritual. Sadly that way of thinking has infiltrated Christianity. It tends to

lead in one of two opposite directions. It can encourage immorality since, if physical things are unimportant, God cannot
be concerned with what we do with our bodies. But it can also
produce an extreme asceticism which encourages us to cut
ourselves off from the material world and deny ourselves
physical pleasures. The really holy person, it is implied, remains celibate and survives on little more than bread and water. That is a denial of the clear teaching of the Bible that everything God created is good. Genesis 1 stresses that point
repeatedly. Three times the writer tells us, "God saw that it was
good" (verses 10, 12 and 18), before his climatic statement at
the end of the sixth day: "God saw all that he had made, and
it was very good" (verse 31).

Sadly, the goodness of creation has been marred by the fall
of Adam and Eve, but it still remains. That is clear from the
words of the apostle Paul when condemning some false teach-
ers who forbade people to marry or eat certain foods: "Everything God created is good, and nothing is to be rejected if it is
received with thanksgiving" (1 Timothy 4:4).

CREATION IS ORDERED

At first "the earth was formless and empty" (Genesis 1:2).
God had created matter but had not yet arranged or orga-
nized it. In the first three days of creation he brought order
to that chaos. On the first day he separated light from darkness (verse 4). On the second he separated the waters of the
heavens (the sky) and the waters of the earth (verse 6). And

on the third day he separated the dry ground from the seas (verse 9). Then, having formed the universe, the earth, the sky and the seas, he filled them. As he did so, he ordered what he made in different categories: "God said, 'Let the land produce vegetation: seed-bearing plants and trees on the land that bear fruit with seed in it, according to their various kinds'" (verse 11). That phrase "according to their various kinds" appears again in verses 21 (twice), 24 and 25. In these separations and different categories we see the order of God's creation. Everything has its place.

It is that order which makes science possible. In the words of Gordon Wenham:

> Genesis 1 provided the intellectual underpinning of the scientific enterprise. Its assumption of unity and order underlying the manifold and seemingly capricious phenomena of experience rests on Genesis 1's assertion of the one almighty God who created and controls the world according to a coherent plan. Only such an assumption can justify the experimental method. Were this world controlled by a multitude of capricious deities, or subject to mere chance, no consistency could be expected in experimental results and no scientific laws could be discovered.[5]

As Johannes Kepler, the founder of modern physical astronomy, said, the early scientists saw themselves as "thinking God's thoughts after him."

·

CREATION IS BEAUTIFUL

"[God] has made everything beautiful in its time" (Ecclesiastes 3:11). That is the testimony of the writer of Genesis 2. He writes: "The LORD God made all kinds of trees grow out of the ground—trees that were *pleasing to the eye* and good for food" (Genesis 2:9, emphasis added). God is not just concerned to make a functional creation that works; he also wants it to be beautiful. He created us with an aesthetic sense and made things of beauty for us to enjoy. We must make sure that we show proper gratitude by appreciating them.

Imagine a woman who puts great effort into decorating a birthday cake for her husband. She spends hours on the icing which depicts a game of football, and even makes sure that the players wear the colors of his favorite team. But he is not interested in what it looks like. As far as he is concerned, a cake is for eating, not viewing, so he dives straight in. His wife is understandably upset.

Are we not like that when we never stop to enjoy and admire the beautiful world our heavenly Father has made for us to live in? Some Christians are such activists that they feel guilty if they are not busy trying to achieve something. Some may even imply that those who make time to walk in God's creation or to appreciate a work of art, a good book or a piece of music are wasting their time. But we are not just machines. God has made a beautiful world. We should be grateful and enjoy it.

CREATION GLORIFIES GOD

Architect Christopher Wren is buried inside his masterpiece, St. Paul's Cathedral. On his tomb a Latin inscription proclaims *Si monumentum requiris circumspice*: "If you are looking for his memorial, look around you." The magnificence of the building proclaims the greatness of the man. In a similar way, God's creation speaks of his great qualities: his power, goodness and splendor. This is the supreme goal of all that exists: to praise and glorify its Creator. The psalmist writes, "The heavens declare the glory of God; / the skies proclaim the work of his hands" (Psalm 19:1). The apostle Paul goes so far as to say that atheism and idolatry are inexcusable. We should all know from the world around us that there is a great Creator, above and beyond all that he made, who demands our gratitude and worship:

> Since the creation of the world God's invisible qualities—his eternal power and divine nature—have been clearly seen, being understood from what has been made, so that men are without excuse. (Romans 1:20)

CREATION IS "UNFINISHED"

All that God made was undoubtedly good from the very beginning, but it was not designed to fulfill its potential on its own. Theologian Christopher J. H. Wright puts it this way: "It is not really biblical to imagine the whole earth at the dawn of human history as a perfect paradise, or that all the forces of nature that we find threatening or unpleasant are the result of human sin and divine curse."[6] There were elements that needed subduing even in God's original creation. God's instruction to human beings to "subdue" the earth (Genesis 1:28) was designed not just to benefit humanity but to bring creation to greater maturity and thus lead to more glory for its Creator.

Tim Chester writes, "The world God made was perfect, but it was not finished. God gave it to us to explore, to enrich, to be creative. . . . The image of gardening captures this idea well. A good gardener works with nature rather than against it, to create from nature something even more beautiful by tending and caring for it."[7]

THE EARTH WAS ENTRUSTED TO HUMAN BEINGS

God's servant-kings. A right understanding of the earth must begin with the truth that it was created by God. But there is another fundamental truth that we also need to grasp: God entrusted the world he made to human beings. Immediately after his creation of men and women, he gave them a clear command: "Be fruitful and increase in number; fill the earth and subdue it. Rule over the fish of the sea and the birds of the air and over every living creature that moves along the ground" (Genesis 1:28).

Some think this command in Genesis 1:28 has produced a contemptuous attitude to the environment which has contributed to the current ecological crisis. They believe it sanctions exploitation without restraint. For example, Ian McHarg has written: "If one seeks licence for those who would increase radioactivity, create canals and harbours with atomic bombs, employ poisons without constraint, or give consent to the bulldozer mentality, there could be no better injunction than this text."[8] It is a serious misreading of God's command in Genesis 1:28, however, to understand it as a charter for abuse. Throughout Genesis 1 we are reminded that God has created a good world. He can hardly be giving humans beings permis sion to destroy it in the very same chapter.

Human beings are part of the created order, and yet as those uniquely made in the image of God, we have been placed over it. We are commanded to "rule" over the rest of God's creatures (Genesis 1:26, 28). This is the language not simply of steward-ship but of kingship. In Christopher Wright's words,

> God here passes on to human hands a delegated form of God's own kingly authority over the whole of his cre-ation. It is commonly pointed out that kings and em-perors in ancient times (and even dictators in modern times) would set up an image of themselves in far-flung corners of their domains to signify their sovereignty over that territory and its people. The image repre-sented the authority of the true king. Similarly, God in-stalls the human species as the image, within creation, of the authority that finally belongs to God, creator and owner of the universe.[9]

As those made in God's image, our dominion over creation should be modeled on the way he exercises his rule as king of the universe. He is a loving king, deeply concerned for the best interests of his subjects. King David exalts "my God the king":

> The LORD is gracious and compassionate,
>   slow to anger and rich in love.
>
> The LORD is good to all;
>   he has compassion on all he has made.
> (Psalm 145:1, 8-9)

This gracious rule of God is exhibited supremely in his Son, the Lord Jesus, who "did not come to be served, but to serve, and to give his life as a ransom for many" (Mark 10:45). The same attitude of service should govern our attitude to creation as we fulfill our responsibilities as God's rulers over it.

As the Creator, God continues to be the owner of all that he has made (Psalm 24:1-2). Just as the Israelite kings were accountable to God for how they exercised their rule, so all human beings, as God's kings over creation, will be accountable to him for how we fulfill that task.

We have no liberty to do what we like with our natural environment; it is not ours to treat as we please. "Dominion" is not a synonym for "domination," let alone "destruction." Since we hold it in trust, we have to manage it responsibly and productively.[10]

TWO TASKS

Our responsibility as God's kings over the earth is spelled out in Genesis 2:15: "The LORD God took the man and put him in the Garden of Eden to work it and take care of it." Christopher Wright reflects on this passage: "The garden of Eden was not the whole planet. It was a safe and bounded environment within the earth into which God put the first humans. The implication of this limited location of Eden and the placing of humans initially within it would seem to be that the task of subduing the earth would begin there and extend outwards into a world as yet far from subdued."[11]

There are two tasks: to "work" the land and to "take care" of it. We are meant to "work" the land, cultivating the soil so that it produces fruit. This command points to a much broader encouragement to develop the resources God has placed in the world so that we can put them to use. It is not long before we find human beings forging tools out of bronze and iron (Genesis 4:22), and after the flood God gives explicit permission for us to eat meat and fish (Genesis 9:2-3).

We are encouraged to work the land. But we are also to "take care" of it. Those words "take care" underline that God is not giving us a free hand to do whatever we want with his creation. We are to exercise a responsible dominion, ensuring that we do not just develop the earth and its resources but also conserve it.

There are striking links between the writer's description of the garden and the tabernacle which Moses was commanded to erect as the focal point of the worship of God. Gold and onyx are prominent in both (Genesis 2:12; Exodus 25:7, 11; 28:6, 9, 13). It is likely that the golden lampstand in the tab-

ernacle was designed to represent the tree of life; and God's
law, represented in the garden by the tree of the knowledge of
good and evil, appears in the tabernacle in the tablets placed
in the ark. It seems we are meant to view Eden as the proto-
typical tabernacle or temple. The Hebrew words translated
"work" and "take care" (Genesis 2:15) are both used later in
the Bible in specifically religious contexts. "Work" is often
used to speak of the service of God—particularly, in some
texts, the service of priests in the tabernacle (Numbers 3:7-8;
4:23-24). "Take care" is also frequently used of religious du-
ties, especially the Levites' task of guarding the tabernacle
(Numbers 1:53; 3:7-8). These links underline the significance
of our responsibilities in creation. When we "work" the earth
and "take care" of it we are engaged in a high calling: the
priestly task of worshiping God.

TWO TASKS (GENESIS 2:15)

- "Work" the earth (development)
- "Take care" of the earth (conservation)

DEVELOPMENT WITHOUT CONSERVATION

It is vital that we give attention to both tasks God has entrusted to us rather than stressing one at the expense of the
other. In recent centuries we have too frequently engaged in
development without sufficient regard to conservation. We
have worked the earth without taking care of it. We have al-

lowed industrialization to march forward without taking enough notice of the effect on the landscape or the environment. In our desperation for profit or energy in the short term we have not paid enough attention to the long-term consequences of our so-called progress. Accidents like the 1984 chemical incident at Bhopal or the 1986 nuclear incident in Chernobyl gave us solemn warnings, but there are few signs that we have taken them as seriously as we should. Meanwhile, deforestation continues at an alarming rate. Each year ten trees are cut down for every one replanted. The result is the loss of half the tropical rainforests of the world. One disturbing consequence of this deforestation is severe soil erosion. "Soil has been so abused in parts of the world that 11% of the world's vegetated soil is beyond recovery—an area the size of China and India."[12]

We are leaving an awful legacy for future generations. But we are not simply stewards of the earth for them. Our ultimate responsibility is to God. We have failed terribly in our God-given task of taking care of the earth for him.

CONSERVATION WITHOUT DEVELOPMENT

We should be careful that we do not respond to these abuses by going to the opposite extreme: conservation without development. Much harm has undoubtedly come from the industrial and technological advances of the last two centuries, but they have also brought much that is good. While acknowledging the dark side, let us also thank God for the positive progress brought by trains, cars, electricity and computers. There are some "eco-warriors" who, like the Luddites of the Industrial Revolution, seem to object to progress of any kind. They oppose every new road, airport or housing development almost without exception. Of course we should take account of the impact of any decision on the environment, but that should be only one factor; it should not be decisive on its own. Our country might be more beautiful if the government forbade all cars and planes, but would it be a better place to live?

What about animal experimentation? Some insist that it can never be right to use other creatures in that way for our advantage. We should certainly be concerned to treat animals well and to minimize their suffering. We should be very reluctant to conduct experiments on them. They are part of God's good creation, of which we have been commanded to take care. But we should also remember that we have been set above the animals. We, alone of all God's creatures, have been made in his image. So, if there is a choice between an animal suffering or a human being, the human has a right priority. There should be strict controls but it surely must be right, for example, that a drug with a possible medical application should be treated on animals first before being given to humans.

And what should be our attitude toward genetic engineering? We are wise to be cautious about genetically modified crops, considering their potentially negative effect on the environment. We must not make the mistakes of the past and forge ahead without paying enough attention to the risks and possible consequences. But, as we take all necessary precautions, let us also remember our responsibility to develop the earth's resources. More than a third of the world's agricultural production is lost to pests and diseases. Genetic engineering has great potential as a means of increasing yields by producing crops resistant to those problems and resilient in the face of drought and frost. Results that take years through normal breeding methods can be produced in weeks through genetic modification. This great potential must not be ignored but should be weighed alongside the concerns.

There are no easy answers. The challenge is to move forward with both development and conservation; working the earth and taking care of it.

WHAT DIFFERENCE CAN I MAKE?

We can be left feeling utterly helpless in the face of the huge issues that face our world. What difference can I make? The answer is very little—on our own. But as more and more individuals make the same point or take the same action, they can have a significant impact.

This is an area in which many in the world are increasingly active, but Christians are often strangely silent and passive. Surely we should be more concerned about the earth than anyone else: it belongs to our heavenly Father, and he has entrusted it to us.

We must ensure that we exercise our responsibility as consumers in a godly way. If more and more of us were to make it clear that we do not want to eat meat produced from animals held in appalling factory conditions, farming practices would change. If we were to prefer fair trade products to others, more would appear on the shelves. And if we were to demand recycling facilities and make sure we used them, shops and local authorities would, in the end, cooperate. In a market economy, the consumer is king.

We should also exercise our responsibilities as voters. As those who live in a democracy, we have the privilege of being able to influence the decisions that are made on our behalf. It is our Christian duty to make the most of that opportunity. Let us ensure that our vote is decided not by our priorities but by God's, which surely include the environment. As we enter the political debate, let us be wary of simplistic rhetoric that ignores the realities of life in less developed countries. A particular environmental policy might appear obvious and essential to us when viewed from the comfort of our prosperous lives, but have we considered what the effect might be on others, not least the poor in other parts of the world? We should be reticent about advocating policies which require other people to change their lifestyles or lose their livelihoods without being willing to face a sacrifice ourselves. We should tell our politicians not only that environmental issues concern us but that we are prepared to pay a price for that concern, both in our own country and by funding significantly increased support for poorer nations.

THE EARTH WILL BE REDEEMED BY CHRIST

Many Christians have a sub-biblical view of salvation. They imagine that it is limited to our "souls" or "spirits." Their vision of heaven is of an insubstantial place inhabited by immaterial souls. But the God who made not just our souls, but our bodies and the whole material world as well, could never be satisfied with that. The fall of humanity had disastrous consequences for the whole of creation and, in his infinite love, God is determined to put everything right: our souls, our bodies, and the material world as well.

THE GROANS OF CREATION

Through his death and resurrection Christ has made it possible for us to be restored to right relationship with his Father. He has already been established at the right hand of God as the ruler of the universe. He now invites us to trust in him so that we might become children of God who inherit his blessings. We can enjoy them partially in this world through the gift of the Holy Spirit, but we will receive most of those blessings only when Christ returns at the end of time. His rule will then be acknowledged by all, judgment will come, and everything will be perfectly renewed.

The apostle Paul tells us that the whole of creation longs for that day. "The creation waits in eager expectation for the sons of God to be revealed." At the moment it is "subjected to frustration." It has not fulfilled its destiny. That is why "the whole creation has been groaning as in the pains of childbirth right

up to the present time." Perhaps, with our increasing awareness of the environmental crisis in the world, we are more at-
tuned to those groans than previous generations. It may be that
as the crisis deepens the groaning will get louder, but it will not
continue forever. Just as labor pains are replaced by great joy
when a baby is born, so the pain of the creation will cease one
day when it is "liberated from its bondage to decay" and is
"brought into the glorious freedom of the children of God"
(Romans 8:19-21). Then, at last, all that spoils the material
world will disappear and a perfect new creation will be born.

THE NEW CREATION IN THE BIBLE

Behold, I will create new heavens and a new earth. (Isaiah
65:17; see also 2 Peter 3:13; Revelation 21:1)

Features of the new creation:

- *Harmony within creation.* "The wolf will live with the lamb,
  / the leopard will lie down with the goat, / the calf and the
  lion and the yearling together; / and a little child will lead
  them. . . . The infant will play near the hole of the cobra, /
  and the young child put his hand into the viper's nest" (Isaiah 11:6-8; see also Isaiah 65:25).

- *Intimacy with God.* "The earth will be full of the knowledge
  of the LORD / as the waters cover the sea" (Isaiah 11:9; see
  also Isaiah 65:24). "Now the dwelling of God is with men,
  and he will live with them. They will be his people, and
  God himself will be with them and be their God. He will
  wipe away every tear from their eyes" (Revelation 21:3-4).

TWO GREAT COMMANDS

Our ultimate home as Christians is the new creation. We are "strangers in the world" (1 Peter 1:1) and "our citizenship is in heaven" (Philippians 3:20). But until Christ returns, we must live here on earth. How should we live in the meantime? Should we be concerned for this present world or for the world to come? The answer must be both, but that is not easy to work out in practice. "The church has always struggled to find and then maintain the right expression of its two-sided calling, to be fully engaged in the world yet with priorities transformed by its own eternal perspective. Like a boat at anchor, the conflicting currents of creation and salvation, of this world and the next, have pulled the church in different directions: first to recognise the importance of the 'natural order' and then to disparage it."[13]

Some Christians imply that we should not really bother with this world, as it will pass away as soon as Christ returns. To get involved in politics or environmental issues is seen as a waste of time, like rearranging deckchairs on the Titanic: If the ship is going down, why fuss about such things? It may be that you share that view. Perhaps you have wondered as you have read this chapter, *Why are we thinking about this subject? Surely evangelism is the only task really worth doing in the light of eternity?* But that cannot be right. Our Redeemer is also our Creator. This material world has value: God made it and is concerned for it. He demonstrated his concern for creation in the most powerful way possible: by sending his Son to redeem it.

God's work of salvation is not a rejection of the material world; it is a renewal of it, as proclaimed by Christ's resurrection. It is our responsibility as Christ's disciples to be concerned for it too and to seek to make it as good a place to live as we possibly can. The creation mandate of Genesis 1:28 still applies. We still have the responsibility to fill the earth and subdue it, to work the land and take care of it.

But as we exercise our God-given stewardship of the world, we must be realistic. This fallen world will always bear the marks of sin until Christ returns. Only he can save the earth. Our creator is also our redeemer. While we wait for the glorious day when he appears to complete his redemptive work, we have another great command to obey. The Lord Jesus has instructed us to "go and make disciples of all nations" (Matthew 28:19), calling on people everywhere to turn from their sin and trust in Christ.

One day, it could even be the day after tomorrow, there will be a disaster more terrible than any film can portray. The whole world will be destroyed as God acts in judgment. But that will not be the end; it will lead to a new world, perfect in every way. It is our privilege and responsibility to warn others of coming judgment and tell them the good news that, despite their sin, they can have a place in God's new creation if they turn to Christ. That new creation is worth waiting for. All God's people will be there, not just as souls but with physical bodies in a physical place (see 1 Corinthians 15). In that day, says the prophet Isaiah,

You will go out in joy
    and be led forth in peace;
the mountains and the hills
    will burst into song before you,
and all the trees of the field
    will clap their hands. (Isaiah 55:12)

The whole creation will join in the worship of God, its Creator and Redeemer.

● BIBLE STUDY: GENESIS 1:26-31; 2:4-17

What is the proper relationship between human beings and the rest of the created order (Genesis 1:26-31)?

Are there any limitations to our "rule"?

What is implied about the contribution human beings can make to the earth (Genesis 2:4-7)?

What does the garden God made (Genesis 2:8-14) teach us about

- God?

- how we should live?

In what ways are we failing in our responsibilities to "work" the earth and "take care" of it (15-17)

- in the world?

- in our own country?

- in our own lives?

Is this a legitimate concern for Christians?

What can we do to make a difference?

4

GOD'S DESIGN FOR SEX AND MARRIAGE

The whirlwind of change in Western society in the last few decades is nowhere more pronounced than in the area of sex and marriage. Statistics tell the tale. In 1965 about a third of eighteen-year-old boys and less than one in five girls of the same age had had sex. A decade later the percentages had more than doubled for boys and tripled for girls.[1] Even more troubling, from 1990 to 2000 in Great Britain, the average number of sexual partners over a lifetime rose from nine to thirteen for men and from four to six and a half for women.[2]

The new sexual permissiveness has had a significant effect on marriage. The percentage of American adults who have gone through a divorce tripled between 1970 and 1994.[3] Births outside marriage were steady in Great Britain at about 4.5 percent throughout the nineteenth century and first half of the twentieth century, except for slight rises during the two world wars. But from the 1970s onward there has been a dramatic increase, with the figure reaching 39 percent by the dawn of the twenty-first century.[4]

It would be wrong to imply that everything was rosy before the arrival of the permissive society. There was a prudish, self-righteous element in the old morality which was often hypocritical, and no doubt individuals did sometimes feel trapped in miserable, even abusive, marriages. But who can deny that the sexual revolution has come with a high price tag attached? Patrick Fagan and Robert Rector report that "each year, over 1 million American children suffer the divorce of their parents; moreover, half of the children born this year to parents who are married will see their parents divorce before they turn 18."[5]

Children are not the only ones to suffer. A family breakup affects grandparents, uncles and aunts as well as the parents and children. There is also an impact on society. It is no exaggeration to say that family breakdown leads to significant societal breakdown. Without strong family life, loneliness and isolation increase, as does dependence on the state. Who else is there to look after you in old age if the family has disintegrated? A substantial part of the next generation is growing up without role models of both genders in the home and never having witnessed at close hand a stable adult relationship. Only time will tell what legacy that produces as they reach adulthood. Many single parents do a remarkable job in very difficult circumstances, but they would often be the first to acknowledge that the ideal would be to raise their child in a two-parent household.

There have never been more sex manuals and relationship counselors, and yet we, as individuals and as a society, have again and again proved ourselves to be ignorant, or at least very foolish, in those areas. There is still a desperate need for guidance, and there is nowhere better to turn for it than to the opening chapters of Genesis. Here we find the voice of our Creator: the Maker's instructions.

THE MAKER'S INSTRUCTIONS

Tony Jones of Claypath Church in Durham, England, suggests the following headings for God's instructions about human sexuality:

- God is for sex

- Sex is for marriage

- Marriage is for life

GOD IS FOR SEX

In the middle ages Yves of Chartres encouraged Christians to abstain from sex on Sundays, in remembrance of the resurrection; Mondays out of respect for departed souls; Thursdays to focus on Christ's rapture; Fridays, as Christ died on that day; and Saturdays in honor of the Virgin Mary.[6] There were not many days left. Such teaching has given the impression that God is antisex. But you will not find anything like that in the Bible. God is for sex; he invented it. Two important themes concerning God's creation design for sex are stressed in Genesis 1: complementarity and reproduction.

Complementarity. "So God created man in his own image, in the image of God he created him; male and female he created them" (Genesis 1:27). God did not create us as androgynous or sexless beings; he made us male and female. As we saw in chapter two, our gender is fundamental to who we are as human beings. We are not just people; we are men and women. God made us equal: both men and women are created in the image of God. Yet we are also different.

In Genesis 2 we find Adam in the wonderful garden God made for him; but all is not well. "The LORD God said, 'It is not good for the man to be alone. I will make a helper suitable for him'" (Genesis 2:18). All the beasts of the field and the birds of the air are then paraded before him. I imagine Adam shaking his head as one by one they are presented to him: an antelope, orangutan, flamingo . . . Each is rejected: "For Adam no suitable helper was found." So God creates one especially for him, and Adam is delighted. He cannot contain his joy when he first sees the woman and cries out: "This is now bone of my bones / and flesh of my flesh; / she shall be called 'woman,' / for she was taken out of man" (Genesis 2:20, 23).

Adam rejoices in Eve's *likeness* to him. Those animals would never do, but here is a fellow human being, "bone of my bones and flesh of my flesh." And yet he is also thrilled that she is *different.* She is a woman, not another man. Thomas Schmidt puts it this way:

Humanity is created male and female (Genesis 1:27). Adam is not given a mirror-image companion, he is given a *her* (Genesis 2:18), and he delights in her *corre-spondence* to him (Genesis 2:23), which resides both in her likeness (human) and her difference (female).[7]

God made men and women not identical but complementary. They are designed for one another. So we are not to lament the differences between men and women. Men and women complement each other so that, in God's creation design, when we come together we are a perfect fit. That fit is not only physical, but it is certainly seen in our bodies. God designed men and women to come together sexually. "The penis fits inside the vagina and the fit is pleasurable to both partners."[8] God is not embarrassed about bodies and sex, nor should we be. Sex is good. Genesis 1 concludes with a delightful description of uninhibited shame-free sexuality: "The man and his wife were both naked, and they felt no shame."

Reproduction. Sex is created as the means of reproduction. God's first commandment to humanity is "Be fruitful and increase in number" (Genesis 1:28), or, in other words, "Have sex! Propagate!" That command appears in the context of the responsibility given to humanity to have dominion over the world God has made. Procreation makes that stewardship and rule possible. Humanity is to be fruitful and increase that they might "fill the earth and subdue it."

By nature we are focused on ourselves. We come to a relationship looking for personal pleasure, security or satisfaction. John Gray's *Men Are from Mars, Women Are from Venus* is the most popular relationship book of recent years. It has a revealing subtitle: *A Practical Guide for Improving Communication and Getting What You Want in Relationships*.[9] By contrast Christopher Ash's book on the Bible's teaching on sex and marriage has as its subtitle: *Sex in the Service of God*.[10] That is God's intention for our relationships. He wants us to focus on him and serve him.

Ash argues that Christians have often drawn the wrong conclusions from the words of Genesis 2:18. A common interpretation is that Adam's chief problem in the garden was loneliness, and that God responded by creating Eve as a companion for him. The goal of marriage is then seen as a mutually satisfying relationship between a man and a woman. That understanding leads to a couple entering their marriage with the introspective primary goal of meeting each others' needs for companionship. That perspective is fueled by the language that is used in much marriage preparation and fulfillment material. One book is subtitled *Achieve a Happy and More Fulfilling Relationship*. A course is subtitled "Developing Closeness in Your Marriage." Another proclaims, "This course offers a blueprint for happiness with your partner."[11]

There is certainly much that is right and good in this. God does intend a husband and wife to delight in each other. But mutual delight was never intended to be the ultimate goal of the relationship. The words of Genesis 2:18 must be understood in context. God has issued the creation mandate: human beings are to "be fruitful and increase in number; fill the earth and subdue it" (Genesis 1:28). In

Genesis 2:15 Adam is placed in the Garden of Eden and commanded "to work it and take care of it." It is immediately after that command that God says, "It is not good for the man to be alone."

The natural thought from the flow of the text, therefore, when we are told that Adam needs a "helper," is that this is connected with the work that he has been given to do. He needs someone to come to his aid for he cannot do this work "alone."[12]

Ash goes on to suggest that "marriage is given to enable humankind to exercise responsible dominion over God's world."[13] So, far from being inward-looking, a married couple should be looking upward to God and outward to the world in which he calls them to serve him. "In the Bible's perspective the way forward is neither via individual autonomy nor introspective companionship, but in the joyful shared service of God."[14]

One of the chief ways in which a couple is called to serve God is by producing and raising children, if he gives them that gift. God's creation mandate begins with the command to "be fruitful and multiply." The earth can be subdued only as new generations are born and raised to fulfill that task as God's servant-kings. But since the fall, human beings have chosen to try to rule the world *instead* of God rather than *under* him. So it is not enough simply for a new generation to be born; they must submit to God's authority.

The main responsibility of Christian parents is to raise disciples who will devote their lives to serving Christ. That goal is far more important than the ambitions the world encourages us to have for our offspring. Parents should take great time and trouble to pray for their children, model the Christian life to them and teach them God's word.

BIRTH CONTROL

If reproduction is an important part of a married couple's service of God, can it ever be right for them to use contraception?

- The Bible does not address this question directly.

- Roman Catholic teaching does not permit "artificial" contraception, believing that sexual intercourse can only be moral if it is open to the possibility of reproduction. (Less technological methods such as the "rhythm" method [the couple restricts intercourse to infertile periods] and *coitus interruptus* [the withdrawal of the male before ejaculation] are permitted in Roman Catholic teaching.)

- Protestant thought allows contraception. The Bible assumes that a married couple will want to have children, but that does not mean that contraception is always inappropriate. As Christopher Ash writes, "There is a principled difference between the use of contraception within marriage in the service of 'planned parenthood' and the use of the same medical contraception techniques within or outside marriage with the explicit and long-term aim of preventing parenthood from happening at all" (page 183 of his *Marriage: Sex in the Service of God*).

SEX IS FOR MARRIAGE

Marriage is God-given. God did not just create sex; he also instituted marriage as the right context for it. The two genders were designed to be different that they might complement one another. The writer of Genesis comments: "For this reason a man will leave his father and mother and be united to his wife, and they will become one flesh" (Genesis 2:24). That verse is quoted by Jesus and Paul (Matthew 19:5; 1 Corinthians 6:16; Ephesians 5:31). It constitutes God's definition of marriage.

SEX IS FOR MARRIAGE

- Marriage is God-given (Genesis 2:24).

- Marriage is exclusive ("A man will leave his father and mother").

- Marriage forms a deep unity ("They will become one flesh").

- Marriage is a picture of the relationship of Christ and his church (Ephesians 5:29-32).

Many see marriage as just a human institution that is now past its sell-by date. Given the proportion of broken marriages, it is hardly surprising that many younger people are either nervous of making such a commitment themselves or cannot see the point of doing so. In a 2003 survey in Great Britain, less than 60 percent of teenagers said they would get married.[15] Increasing numbers choose to live together instead.

But we dismiss marriage at our peril. It is not just a piece of paper; it is God-given. Marriage was instituted by our Creator as the proper context for a sexual relationship between a man and a woman.

Marriage is exclusive. The Bible's foundational words about marriage begin by saying, "A man will leave his father and mother." That obviously does not mean a bride and groom should end all contact with their parents. Nevertheless, marriage does mark a decisive break. Previously the main social unit for the couple had been the families of their birth. But from the wedding day onward the relationship with husband or wife is to take precedence.

Too many relationships are put under pressure by in-laws who do not accept that fact and will not give the married couple sufficient space, or by a husband or wife who has never really left the old home and is always going back to Mom or Dad, whether physically or emotionally. That must stop; there does need to be a break. The relationship with parents should never be quite the same again after marriage. It is because parents rightly sense that necessity that weddings can be fraught with all sorts of mixed emotions, including love and joy as well as grief and jealousy.

This exclusive relationship of marriage is between one man and one woman. There are examples of polygamy in the Bible, but they are only described, not commended. The narrative frequently indicates what damage they cause. Once they are married, a couple should not marry anyone else; neither are they to have sex with anyone else. They are to be faithful, "forsaking all others." The writer of Proverbs urges us:

Drink water from your own cistern,
running water from your own well.
Should your springs overflow in the streets,
your streams of water in the public squares?
Let them be yours alone,
never to be shared with strangers.
May your fountain be blessed,
and may you rejoice in the wife of your youth.
A loving doe, a graceful deer—
may her breasts satisfy you always,
may you ever be captivated by her love.
Why be captivated, my son, by an adulteress?
Why embrace the bosom of another man's wife?
(Proverbs 5:15-20)

Marriage forms a deep unity. In marriage a man is "united to his wife" and they "become one flesh" (Genesis 2:24). Although, as we have seen, the creation of a deep relationship is not in itself the goal of marriage, it is part of God's plan. He created sex not just for reproduction but for relationship. It is designed not only to produce children but to bind a man and a woman together in marriage. The words "one flesh" speak of a profound union that exists at every level of their being. That one-flesh union is established, expressed and strengthened by their bodily union.

In God's creation design, sex is profoundly relational. But in our culture it is increasingly seen not relationally but recreationally, as a means to individual pleasure. This *Playboy/Sex in the City* mentality offers much but ultimately never satisfies. It is dehumanizing, seeking a pleasure rather than a person. Once it has had what it wants it quickly moves on, pausing only to mark another notch on the bedpost. After all, as C. S. Lewis put it, "One does not keep the carton after one has smoked the cigarettes."[16] It is no wonder that the permissive society has left so many lonely, hurting people in its wake; they feel used.

It may be that our culture is beginning to recognize the damage caused by such a low view of sex. *Cosmopolitan* magazine has long been associated with a "go-get-it-girl" approach to sex. But there was a striking change of tone in a 2003 edition. The editor comments on the emotional damage caused to women who move from partner to partner. She calls it "soulless sex" or "McSex"—"the takeaway coupling that leaves you feeling empty." A social psychologist is quoted: "There have been some misguided assumptions linked to the sexual revolution and one is that sex can be both casual and happy. In human beings sex is usually linked to an emotional bond, and without that it is at best unsatisfactory, but at worst humiliating and degrading."[17] That is exactly what Genesis 2 would lead us to expect. Sex was designed not for selfish pleasure but to bind a couple together in the committed relationship of marriage.

Marriage is a picture of the relationship of Christ and his church. The apostle Paul quotes Genesis 2:24 and comments, "This is a profound mystery—but I am talking about Christ and the church" (Ephesians 5:32). He is saying that the fundamental relationship is that between Christ and his people. There is no deeper, more profound marriage than that. The marriage of a man and a woman is just a shadow of the marriage between Christ and his church. It is not that human marriage provides a useful illustration for Bible writers to use to speak of the relationship between God and his people; it is the other way round. The relationship between Christ and his church comes first; human marriage is patterned on it. That underlines the importance of faithfulness. God is absolutely committed to his relationship with his church. He never breaks his promises, and he expects the same commitment in our marriages with one another.

What about premarital sex? Many people accept the importance of faithfulness within marriage but see nothing wrong with sex before that commitment has been made, especially if it is in the context of a loving relationship. But how do they know it is loving? In one survey 40 percent of girls who had had sex under the age of sixteen said they were in love at the time, but only 6 percent of boys said the same.[18] That suggests there are many disillusioned and, no doubt, deceived girls.

Sex is designed to act as a glue that binds a couple together in lifelong union, and it is very good at the job. That explains why it hurts so much when a couple who have been in a sexual relationship split up. In the film *Vanilla Sky* the characters played by Cameron Diaz and Tom Cruise are together for a brief period before he begins to distance himself from her. She tries to hold on to him, saying, "When you have sex with someone your body makes promises even if you don't." Many share that instinctive awareness that sex can never be simply a bodily transaction without significance. Sex is designed by God to be the body language of lifelong union. So if two people are not prepared to commit themselves in marriage, they should not have sex. If they do, they are saying with their bodies what they are not prepared to say with their lives, and in the end they are likely to get hurt.

Perhaps this applies especially to cohabitation. The pain of a breakup is magnified if a couple has been living together. Cohabitation requires all the emotional demands of marriage but without the security, because no promises have been made. It does not even function as an effective preparation for marriage. Statistics show that those who cohabit before getting married are far more likely to get divorced in the following five years than those who have lived apart. Experience shows that God's way is best; it is for our good. Sex is for marriage.

What about homosexuality? Is God ever in favor of homosexual sex? The Bible's answer is a very clear "no." Homosexual practice is only ever mentioned negatively. That consistent position flows out of the creation base to the Bible's sexual morality provided by Genesis 1—2. It is to creation that Paul refers when he speaks of homosexual sex as "unnatural" (Romans

1:26-27). God's gift of sex was designed to be the means of re-production within the complementary relationship of a man and a woman. Biology tells us that, and the Bible assumes that it is not an accident of nature. It is God's creation design and has moral significance. We are called to serve God with our bodies (Romans 12:1-2; 1 Corinthians 6:20), and "the activities of our bodies must agree with the way we were made."[19]

How should we respond to those who insist that homosexuality is entirely "natural" to them: "God made us this way"? Richard Kirker, the general secretary of the British Gay and Lesbian Christian Movement, has said, "It would be a very cavalier and capricious God who created people in a certain way and then instructed them that they are forbidden from fulfilling all the potential they have been given."[20]

It is undoubtedly true that some people are attracted predominantly or exclusively to the same sex, either for a period of time or throughout their lives. It seems that these feelings are prompted by a range of different factors which vary from person to person. Whatever their cause, it is clear from the Bible that same-sex attraction is not part of God's creation design and should therefore not be expressed physically.

Perhaps this is a very personal issue for you. If so, talk to a trusted friend or pastor about it. You should not feel guilty just because of the feelings you have. Since the fall every part of us has been marred, including our sexuality. It is hard for all of us to resist sexual temptation, and we need to help each other.

We must continue to uphold the clear teaching of the Bible

that sex is only for heterosexual marriage. But at the same time, we should acknowledge that we all find it difficult to obey this teaching and, in our different ways, often fail. None of us is in a position to look down on anyone else in this area. Do we ensure that our church is one in which individuals are able to admit to failure and their need of help? Would those struggling with homosexuality feel that they could share this with someone, confident of their understanding, love and support? We all need the encouragement of others to obey the Bible's teaching that sex is only for marriage.

MARRIAGE IS FOR LIFE

In Matthew 19, Jesus quotes from Genesis 1—2 and acknowl-edges what is written as the voice of the Creator. Some Phari-sees ask him, "Is it lawful for a man to divorce his wife for any and every reason?" He replies,

> Haven't you read . . . that at the beginning the Creator "made them male and female," and said, "For this reason a man will leave his father and mother and be united to his wife, and the two will become one flesh"? So they are no longer two, but one. Therefore what God has joined together, let man not separate. (Matthew 19:3-6)

Marriage is not just a human contract. God is involved wherever the ceremony is performed and whether the couple is conscious of making their vows before him or not. He has joined them together, and he expects them to stay together.

James Dobson quotes some striking words his father spoke to his mother before their marriage and then wrote down:

> I want you to understand and be fully aware of my feelings concerning the marriage covenant which we are about to enter. I have been taught at my mother's knee, and in conformity to the word of God, that the marriage vows are inviolable, and by entering into them I am binding myself absolutely and for life. The idea of estrangement from you through divorce through any reason at all will never, at any time, be permitted to enter my thinking. I'm not naive on this. On the contrary I am fully aware of the possibility, unlikely as it now appears, that mutual incompatibility or other unforeseen circumstances could result in extreme mental suffering. If such becomes the case I am resolved, for my part, to accept it as a consequence of the commitment I am now making, and to bear it, if necessary, to the end of our lives together.[21]

Those words are out of tune with how many people think today. As they make their vows, they mean to keep them and hope the relationship will last. But they acknowledge, in the back of their minds at least, that if things get difficult they can always leave the marriage and start again with someone else. One advertisement proudly, but sadly, proclaims "statistically, people change their marriage partner before they change their Miele washing machine."[22] We live in a fallen world; there is no perfect marriage. There are bound to be tensions and difficult periods when two sinful human beings are joined together, but that is not a reason to give up. Marriage is designed by God to be for life: "What God has joined together, let man not separate."

The Pharisees react to what Jesus says by referring to Moses' provision for divorce in the Old Testament law. Surely that is a divine sanction for the practice? Jesus replies: "'Moses permitted you to divorce your wives because your hearts were hard. But it was not this way from the beginning" (Matthew 19:7-8). The Old Testament law should not be seen as supporting divorce; it was a concession because of human sin. Jesus continues, "I tell you that anyone who divorces his wife, except for marital unfaithfulness, and marries another woman commits adultery" (Matthew 19:9). We will leave the exception to one side for a moment and focus on the stark general principles: Jesus forbids both divorce and remarriage. Paul summarizes his teaching with these words: "A wife must not separate from her husband. But if she does, she must remain unmarried or else be reconciled to her husband. And a husband must not divorce his wife" (1 Corinthians 7:10-11). The basic principle is very clear: marriage is for life. The disciples are so struck by the commitment involved in Jesus' pronouncement that they say, "If this is the situation between a husband and a wife, it is better not to marry" (Matthew 19:10). Jesus does not agree with them, but he also does not deny that he is setting a very high standard.

"Except for marital unfaithfulness." Jesus forbids divorce

"except for marital unfaithfulness" (Matthew 19:9). Christians differ as to how they understand these words, which do not appear in parallel passages in Mark 10:11 and Luke 16:18. Many see them as permission for both divorce and remarriage if a spouse has been unfaithful. Others disagree. Some point out that the word translated "sexual immorality" is not the usual word for adultery. They believe it refers to a relationship which is forbidden because it is with a close relative. Such a "marriage" should not have been allowed in the first place and should be nullified. Others argue that Jesus is allowing divorce only if a spouse has been unfaithful, but is not allowing for remarriage.

You should refer to other books if you wish to take a closer look at the arguments regarding divorce.[23] Whatever view we take on this disputed matter, we must never forget the basic principle: marriage is meant to be for life. We should be clear about that when we make our marriage vows and be determined to keep them, however hard that may sometimes be.

It may be that you are conscious of having failed in this area already. If so, remember the gospel. It speaks of a loving God who accepts us as we are and forgives us through the death of Christ. We all look back on things we deeply regret in our lives, but no matter how low we might have sunk, the Lord can lift us up. He does not expect us to be perfect when we come to him. He takes us as we are, and as we look to the Holy Spirit for help, he can transform us and use us.

A word for the unmarried. Perhaps you are unmarried but

long to be married one day. If so, the Bible affirms you in that desire. Marriage is a good gift of God. Commit your longing to the Lord and pray for his provision of the right partner at the right time, if that is his will. In your desire to be married, make sure that you do not make a hasty, unwise decision. If you think you might have met the right person, think, pray and seek advice. Marriage is a lifelong commitment, and in the words of the Church of England's wedding service, "it must not be undertaken carelessly, lightly, or selfishly, but reverently, responsibly, and after serious thought."[24]

Some people choose to be single; others find singleness very difficult. As one male friend of mine has put it, "I'm single by choice: the women's choice." Either way, let us make sure we trust God with our lives and do not resent our current circumstances. The Bible affirms both marriage and singleness as gifts of God. Both present different challenges and different opportunities.

A word for the married. If a marriage is to remain strong over many years it will need time and effort. Do not take your marriage for granted. Give time to one another, and express your love both physically and with words. If you are going through a tough time, do not ignore it. Talk to one another and, if it would help, involve someone else you can trust. And talk to God. He bound you together in the first place, so it must be right to pray that he would strengthen that bond. Are you still praying with your husband or wife?

SINGLENESS

While assuming that most will get married, the New Testament also speaks positively about singleness:

1. *Singleness is a gift from God.* "Each man has his own gift from God; one has this gift, another has that" (1 Corinthians 7.7, see also Matthew 19:11). The word *gift* does not refer to a special ability to be married or single; it rather refers to the state of marriage or singleness. All who are single have God's gift of singleness. Some have it for life; others exchange it for the gift of marriage.

2. *There are advantages in being single.* Single people are spared the "troubles" of marriage (1 Corinthians 7:28); single people are able to devote themselves to God's work (1 Corinthians 7:32-35).

3. *No Christian is single forever.* Human marriages will not last for eternity (Mark 12:25). The only marriage in God's perfect future world will be that between Christ and his people. Christians enjoy some of the blessings of that relationship now by the Holy Spirit but will one day enjoy it to the full when Christ returns (Revelation 19:7). That prospect should be an encouragement to all of us, especially to those who struggle with singleness or an unhappy marriage.

Couples will also need to keep ensuring that their primary goal in marriage is to serve God. Husbands, are you fulfilling your responsibility to your wife in your joint service of God? Wives, are you seeking to help and support your husband? It may be that this is not the right time to be starting a family, but are you taking seriously God's desire for "godly off-spring" (Malachi 2:15)? And are you giving enough time, prayer and attention to raising your children as those who put Christ first?

A warning to the proud. Perhaps you have read this chapter with a degree of pride. You have not had sex before marriage and are not committing adultery. As far as you are concerned, it is other people who are the sexual sinners. But is that really true? Jesus said, "Anyone who looks at a woman lustfully has already committed adultery with her in his heart" (Matthew 5:28). We have all sinned sexually, whether in thought or in deed. If there are certain things we have not done, that is only by the grace of God. There is no room for complacency. God's Word warns us: "If you think you are standing firm, be careful that you don't fall!" (1 Corinthians 10:12).

An encouragement to the penitent. It may be that you are very conscious that you have failed in this area. If so, remember that Christ came for sinners. The apostle Paul was uncompromising in his warnings about sin—including sexual sin:

> Do you not know that the wicked will not inherit the kingdom of God? Do not be deceived: Neither the sexually immoral nor idolaters nor adulterers nor male prostitutes nor homosexual offenders nor thieves nor the greedy nor drunkards nor slanderers nor swindlers will inherit the kingdom of God. (1 Corinthians 6:9-10)

If we are engaged in such sinful behavior, we need to repent. If we do, the gospel brings great encouragement. Paul continues:

> And that is what some of you were. But you were washed, you were sanctified, you were justified in the name of the Lord Jesus Christ and by the Spirit of our God. (1 Corinthians 6:11)

If we have turned to Christ, we can be sure that he has already taken the punishment for all the wicked things we have done. They have been dealt with on the cross and will never be counted against us by God. Christ took our sin and has given us his righteousness. We are perfectly clean in God's sight, washed by the blood of Christ. As his people, we can be sure that he will never let us go. Even if we are not faithful to him, he will always keep his promises to us. We have been brought into a perfect marriage that not even death can end.

● BIBLE STUDY: 1 CORINTHIANS 6:12-20

What wrong thinking about sexual behavior did Paul have to counter (vv. 12-13)?

In what ways do we see similar attitudes today?

What does Paul teach us about our bodies? How should these truths affect our sexual behavior (vv. 13-19)?

What will it mean in practice for us to

- "flee from sexual immorality" (v. 18)?
- "honor God with your body" (v. 20)?

How should we try to promote God's standards for sexual morality in the world?

What message(s) does the Bible have for those who have sinned sexually?

GOD'S DESIGN FOR WORK

What do the following have in common: farmer, soldier, king, athlete, lawyer and pastor? They are, in chronological order, the six jobs I set my heart on from childhood through to university. From our very earliest days we are asked, "What are you going to do when you grow up?" In global terms, of course, if we have a choice of what work we will do, we are among the privileged few. Most take whatever job they can get. Many, sadly, can't find any employment. But, assuming we are able to choose a job, work still raises many questions; perhaps more than previous generations had to face.

The world of employment has changed. My father retired having spent over forty years in the same job. That was quite common for his generation but it is increasingly rare these days. None of us can assume we have a job for life anymore. Even if our position is secure, we are increasingly encouraged not to stay in one place but instead to develop a career portfolio, showing experience in different fields. The big decision concerning which job I should do is no longer settled early in life; it is always there, demanding constant review.

Another significant change in the world of work in recent decades has been the number of women in paid employment. This change presents many questions for people to face. Those women or men who choose to stay at home to devote themselves to raising a family are increasingly rare and can be made to feel inadequate. As a result they begin to ask, "Should I go out to work after all?" Parents who do have jobs are more conscious than ever of the difficulty of balancing work and family responsibility.

Our questions are not limited to what job we should do and how much time we should devote to it. We also have many questions about how we should behave when we are at work. How should we respond to the various ethical issues that emerge? What ambitions should we have? What should be our attitude toward work? On the one hand, we find some of our colleagues having a very low view of the job they do: it is just a means to an end. On the other hand, some live for their work: it is the be-all and end-all of life. How should a Christian think?

Does the Bible have anything to say on this vital subject of work? You might not think so if you examined the teaching programs of many churches (I was certainly ashamed when I looked at our church's catalog of recordings recently). One writer has commented:

The average person spends anywhere from 40-75% of

his life in work or work-related tasks. . . . He spends another 30% or 35% on his family and personal interests.
And perhaps he spends as much as 5% or 10% on
church or religious activities. Yet most Christian teaching addresses those areas in precisely the opposite pro-
portions: a very heavy emphasis on religious matters,
some help in regard to marriage and family, but little that
speaks directly to the workplace.[1]

It is no wonder that "every day millions of workers go to
work without seeing the slightest connection between what
they do all day and what they think God wants done in the
world."[2] That must be wrong. God is the great Creator of all
things. As such he is concerned with every part of life. The
Dutch theologian and politician Abraham Kuyper once said,
"There is not one inch of the entire creation about which Jesus
Christ does not cry out, 'This is mine! This belongs to me!'"[3]
That includes our work.

By *work* I do not just mean paid employment. Work is our
productive activity in any sphere of life, whether in a paid job
or in parenting, volunteering in the community, going to
school or doing housework. The Bible has much to say on the
subject of work. As with the other subjects in this book, we
will see again that the foundations of its teaching appear in
Genesis 1—2, which challenges the false views of our culture
with its tendency either to degrade or to deify work. Work
must not be degraded: it is a good part of God's creation. Nor
should it be deified: it is not the goal of life.

GOD'S DESIGN FOR WORK

- Work is a good part of God's creation
- Work is not the goal of life

WORK IS A GOOD PART OF GOD'S CREATION

"Live for the weekend." As far as many are concerned, there is
nothing good about work. It is a necessary evil separating one
weekend from another. They take no satisfaction from it and
just do the bare minimum so that they can pay for their leisure
time. That was the attitude of most of my colleagues when I
worked for a few months in an office. When they arrived at
work in the morning they would focus first on the coffee
break, then lunch time and then clocking out in the afternoon.
Throughout the week, the ultimate goal was five o'clock Friday afternoon. You could almost hear the collective sigh of re-
lief: "Thank God it's Friday!" That attitude was summarized in
a bank slogan: "Live for the weekend."

Is work "unspiritual?" For some, the problem with work is
simply that it is not leisure; that is what they live for. Others
degrade work by viewing it as somehow "unspiritual."

The roots of that attitude are found in the classical world.
Work, especially manual labor, was seen as base and demeaning. The Stoic philosopher Cicero wrote, "The toil of a hard
worker, who is paid only for his toil and not for artistic skill, is
unworthy of a free man and is sordid in character."[4] There has

never been quite such a low view in Christian thinking, but there has been a long tradition that divides different functions in life between the sacred and the secular and ranks them accordingly. Eusebius, bishop of Caesarea in the fourth century, distinguished between two ways of life we can choose as Christians: the "perfect life" or a life that is merely "permitted."

> The perfect life is spiritual, dedicated to contemplation and reserved for priests, monks and nuns; the permitted life is secular, dedicated to action and open to such tasks as soldiering, governing, farming, trading and raising families.[5]

Similar attitudes still linger in Christian circles today. We can be made to feel that we are wasting our time running a business, working in an office or doing housework. If we were really spiritual, it is implied, we would be pastors or missionaries. Such thinking degrades much of our work and implies that it is hardly worth doing. But Christians who affirm the doctrine of creation cannot think like that. If God made the world and everything in it, there can be no division between the secular and the spiritual, the earthly and the sacred. God is concerned with all of life, including our work.

God is a worker. Like everything else, work has been spoiled by human sin, but it is not a product of the fall. Work is one of the features of God's creation which he declared to be "very good" (Genesis 1:31).

The Bible begins by describing not God's leisure but his activity. He is busy in the great work of creation. Having created, he does not relax and do nothing. God is still at work upholding and sustaining the world he has made. We should notice in passing that no one pays God for his work. Labor does not have to be paid to be of value. That should be an encouragement to those who are busy at home, students, unemployed or actively retired. Jesus was a carpenter until the age of thirty. No one paid him for his work of salvation although, in the end, it cost him everything. In his public ministry he often referred to his work: "My food . . . is to do the will of him who sent me and to finish his work" (John 4:34). God dignifies work by being a worker himself.

We human beings have been made in the image of God, and just as he works, he calls us to work too. The account of the creation of the first humans is followed immediately by a command to them to work: "Be fruitful and increase in number; fill the earth and subdue it" (Genesis 1:28). Then in Genesis 2:15 Adam is put in the Garden of Eden to "work it and take care of it." There is work to be done both in the world (subduing the earth and taking care of it) and in the home (being fruitful and raising families). We human beings were not made to be creatures of leisure; we were designed to work. Mark Greene writes, "Work is not an intermission from the main action, something we do so we can then do other things: it is an integral part of the main action, an intrinsic part of our walk with God."[6]

God's coworkers. We are very familiar with the concept of us being God's coworkers in the work of salvation. Salvation rests entirely on the eternal will of God the Father, the sacrificial death of God the Son, and the regenerating work of God the Spirit. Conversion is God's work from start to finish. But he still calls for our cooperation in it. In his sovereignty he has chosen to use us: it is only as we pray and proclaim the gospel that people are saved.

The same principle is at work in God's ordering of creation. He created the Garden of Eden, but he gave man the responsibility of cultivating it: "the first partnership."[7] God did not design this world to be productive on its own. His plans for his creation depend on us for their completion. Martin Luther pointed out: "God gives the wool, but not without our labour. If it is on the sheep, it makes no garment."[8] God provides our daily bread, but he does so using the farmer, the baker, the truck driver and the shopkeeper. "God is the creator; man is the cultivator. Each needs the other. In God's good purpose creation and cultivation, nature and nurture, raw materials and human craftsmanship go together."[9]

Work is spiritual. In light of the truths that God himself is a worker and has created us to be his coworkers, we dare not dismiss work as merely a necessary evil, or "unspiritual." It can sometimes seem as if we operate by the dictum "All Christians are equal, but some are more equal than others."[10] We have a hierarchy of jobs in our minds: missionaries at the top, then other gospel workers, followed perhaps by those in the caring professions or education, and on it goes right down to lawyers at the bottom. But we need to understand that all work is spiritual (with the exception of tasks that are ungodly by definition, such as the work of a thief or a prostitute). We are all called to be full-time Christian workers. We should see our work, whether at home or elsewhere, paid or unpaid, as an important sphere of our Christian service. There is no such thing as "secular work." This understanding "opens the way to regard work not simply as the arena *within which* one serves God but *through which* one serves him."[11] We are not just serving God in our diligence, honesty or witness at work; we serve him in the work itself.

God created us to be workers, and as we work we are helping him fulfill his purposes for his world. If we understood that truth, it would surely transform our attitude toward our work. Sometimes we can feel that it is a waste of time. Some Christians imply that the only worthwhile activity, in the light of eternity, is evangelism. Work is seen as just a meaningless drudge. But a right understanding of the Bible will not allow us to think like that. Work is a vital part of God's plan for us on the earth. He chooses to work out his good purposes for the world through us. In Luther's words, if we thought rightly, "the entire world would be full of service to God, not only the churches but also the home, the kitchen, the cellar, the workshop, and the field."[12]

> God will be working all things through you, he will be milking the cows through you and will be performing the most menial duties through you, and all duties, from the greatest to the least, will be pleasing to him.[13]

The fact that all work is spiritual is wonderfully liberating. We need not feel ashamed any more that our job is not sufficiently "Christian." We can serve God whatever work we do. That truth should also free us from guilt, the kind that is especially common among parents. They are so busy feeding throughout the night and throughout the day, changing diapers and ferrying children here, there and everywhere that they do not have the time or energy they used to have to study the Bible or get involved in programs at church. As they look at some of their other friends who still read the Bible and pray for one hour every day and are at church meetings two evenings a week, they think to themselves: *I'm not doing enough for the Lord.* But we are not serving Christ only when we are at church or have a Bible open in front of us. Parenting is Christian service; it is a job entrusted to mothers and fathers by God. That is true of all our work.

It is said that Ruth Bell Graham had a plaque above the kitchen sink at home which said, "Divine service conducted here three times daily." Perhaps it would help if you imagined such a plaque above your desk, in the library, as a screen saver on your computer or on the oven: "Divine worship offered here." The apostle Paul wrote to some slaves: "Whatever you do, work at it with all your heart, as working for the Lord, not for men" (Colossians 3:23).

Work should be fulfilling. There will always be an element of frustration in our work in this fallen world. When God passed judgment on Adam he said:

> Cursed is the ground because of you;
>> through painful toil you will eat of it
>> all the days of your life.
> It will produce thorns and thistles for you,
>> and you will eat the plants of the field.
> By the sweat of your brow
>> you will eat your food
> until you return to the ground,
>> since from it you were taken;
> for dust you are
>> and to dust you will return. (Genesis 3:17-19)

We still suffer from that sentence today. There is no such thing as perfect job satisfaction this side of heaven. But alongside the frustration, there should be a sense of fulfillment. The key to that fulfillment is not supremely the satisfaction that comes from getting a job done, gaining promotion or earning a large salary. It is rather the knowledge that all our work has value when it is done in God's service and for the good of others.

Sometimes it is easy to see how our work serves God's purposes in the world, but it is harder with other jobs. What use is a student's essay, especially when it is on some obscure subject with no possible practical application? But the training of our minds is an important activity in and of itself. I have never practiced law, but I am very grateful for my two years of legal studies. They taught me how to think. That has proved very useful in all sorts of ways since.

What about the artist or the actor? It is true that their work is not essential; we could get by without it. But God is not interested in producing just a functional world. As we have seen, he created trees that were "pleasing to the eye" (Genesis 2:9). Some jobs are not necessary, but they add to the quality of life by bringing pleasure or intellectual stimulation.

What about workers on an assembly line? It may be very hard for them to see the value of their work. They contribute just one cog in a very large machine. But if they can look beyond the detail of their task to the end product, they should be able to see how they are contributing to the good of God's world. The story is told of a conversation in a medieval stone masons' yard. A visitor asked three masons what they were doing. The first said, "I'm cutting a stone." The second answered, "I'm earning my living." But the third held his head high and said, "I'm building a cathedral." John Stott summarizes this story: "He looked beyond his tools and his wages to the ultimate end he was serving."[11]

Is that how we view our work? If we have the right vision, we should be able to recognize that, in our small way, we are contributing to the work of the divine Creator. He is overseeing the world that it might function as well as a fallen world can function, so that it becomes an arena of praise and worship for his glory.

WORK IS NOT THE GOAL OF LIFE

The cult of careerism. A man found it impossible to tell his wife,

children or friends after he was fired from his job. He contin-
ued to leave home at the usual time as if everything was normal, but instead of going to the office, he spent the day in the
library. That carried on for as long as he had enough savings
in the bank to continue the pretense. When the money ran
out, he shot himself. His work was everything to him. His
sense of identity and self-respect was bound up with it. When
he lost his job, he lost his life.[15]

"I am what I do" is the unstated assumption of many. Career
is allowed to replace God at the center of life. It is where many
look for satisfaction and meaning; everything else is subservi-
ent. I was struck by a title when browsing in a bookstore: *The
Gospel According to the Harvard Business School.*[16] The book offers, in effect, a new religion: the cult of careerism. Its opening
words proclaim:

> This is a book about people who want to get to the top
> of the world. People who are determined that in their
> profession nobody is going to do or be better, and who
> are prepared to pay any price to live up to their expecta-
> tions.

Many live like that. They pay a heavy price for their worship of work. Men and women are willing to sacrifice their
marriage, children, even God himself on the altar of career.
Nothing must be allowed to stand in the way of their march
to the top. It is idolatry. Career is allowed to take the place that
only God should have at the center of our lives.

God's sabbath rest. Just as Genesis 1—2 corrects degrading views of work, it also condemns the deification of work. Work is not the goal of life.

It is a pity that those who divided the Bible into chapters ended Genesis 1 at verse 31, after the creation of human beings and the command to work. The first creation narrative does not end there; its climax comes not with the creation of man and woman on the sixth day but with God's rest on the seventh day:

> By the seventh day God had finished the work he had been doing; so on the seventh day he rested from all his work. And God blessed the seventh day and made it holy, because on it he rested from all the work of creating that he had done. (Genesis 2:2-3)

There is a clear pattern right through Genesis 1, with the same phrases appearing in the description of each day. The first six days all end with the words "and there was evening and there was morning—the first [then second, etc.] day." We are expecting the same words with the seventh day, but they do not come; the seventh day never ends. The work of creation is complete, so God continues to enjoy his sabbath rest.

This does not mean that God is doing nothing. He remains busy with the task of sustaining the world. *Rest* in this context does not imply total inactivity. It is a more positive word that speaks of peace, satisfaction and enjoyment. Having completed his work of creation, God delighted in it. And, wonderfully, he wants us human beings to enjoy his seventh day, his sabbath rest, with him. That is what we see described in Genesis 2.

The seventh day continues. Adam and Eve enjoy life in God's creation in the way it was designed to be lived. They are sharing in God's "rest." They work in the garden, certainly, but the prime focus of their existence is not the job God has entrusted to them but their relationship with him. The central importance of that relationship is symbolized by the two trees right at the heart of the garden: the tree of life and the tree of the knowledge of good and evil (Genesis 2:9). God speaks to them by his word and defines what is right and wrong, good and evil. As they respond to this word with trust and obedience, they enjoy fullness of life in loving fellowship with their Creator. That, ultimately, is what life is all about: not work, but a relationship with God. I like the answer of a man who, when asked on a train platform "Who are you?" replied, "I am a Christian, thinly disguised as an accountant."[17] He recognized that the most significant truth about him was his relationship with God. Compared to that, the particular job he did was insignificant.

The sabbath command. The seventh day at the beginning of Genesis 2 formed the basis of the fourth commandment given to Moses on Mount Sinai:

> Remember the Sabbath day by keeping it holy. Six days you shall labor and do all your work, but the seventh day is a Sabbath to the LORD your God. On it you shall not

do any work, neither you, nor your son or daughter, nor your manservant or maidservant, nor your animals, nor the alien within your gates. For in six days the LORD made the heavens and the earth, the sea, and all that is in them, but he rested on the seventh day. Therefore the LORD blessed the Sabbath day and made it holy. (Exodus 20:8-11)

Does the fourth commandment mean that it is our duty as Christians to avoid work of any kind on Sunday, or at least on one day of every week? Are we sinning if we write an essay, go to the office or even mow the lawn on that day? This is a subject on which Christians disagree.[18] Some believe that the sabbath command is a creation ordinance (Genesis 2:1-3; Exodus 20:11), and so it still applies to Christians today. They believe we sin if we fail to take a complete day off each week. Because the command is fulfilled in Christ, they argue that Christians should rest on Sundays, not Saturdays, to remember Jesus' resurrection, which inaugurated the new creation. Others point out that this sabbath command is never reaffirmed in that way in the New Testament. They believe Christians have freedom in this area. This is my view. As Paul wrote to the Colossians:

Therefore do not let anyone judge you by what you eat or drink, or with regard to a religious festival, a New Moon celebration or a Sabbath day. These are a shadow of the things that were to come; the reality, however, is found in Christ. (Colossians 2:16-17; see also Romans 14:5)

All agree that the supreme way in which we are to fulfill the sabbath command is to come to Christ. He said, "Come to me, all who are weary and burdened, and I will give you *rest*" (Matthew 11:28, emphasis added). The writer to the Hebrews, speaking of God's sabbath rest, says, "Now we who have believed enter that rest" (Hebrews 4:3). It is by coming to Jesus that we enter into God's seventh day and begin to live life again as it was designed to be lived. We can enjoy a taste even now of "Genesis 2 land" while we wait for its perfect restoration at the return of Christ, when all God's original purposes for his creation will be fulfilled.

The fact that the sabbath has been fulfilled in Christ does not mean we can just ignore the fourth commandment. That command underlines the truth that work is not the goal of life. It stresses the importance of rest, remembrance and rescue.

1. Rest. God refers back to creation when he gives the sabbath command to Moses: "For in six days the LORD made the heavens and the earth." The pattern of six days' work followed by one day's rest was established by God at the very beginning. Even if we are not commanded as Christians to rest one day in seven, we are certainly wise to do so. As those made in God's image, we are designed to take a break every seventh day. If we do not, we are liable to break down, whether physically or psychologically. Sadly, many can testify to that fact in our stress-driven, workaholic society.

God may have created us to work, but he never intended us to do so day in, day out. Far from feeling guilty about resting and enjoying leisure time, we should ensure that we build it into our daily and weekly routine: it is God's will. Warning bells should be ringing if we find we are unable to switch off from our work. That suggests we are not taking enough time off. God instituted the sabbath day in the Old Testament not just to point to Christ but to provide a much-needed day of rest for his people.

A day of rest is almost always possible with a bit of planning. It might mean staying late in the office the day before, or starting the essay earlier than usual, but it is worth it. For some people that will be very difficult. For example, when does a parent's work ever stop? But it must at least be possible to take one day at a slower pace and a change of rhythm, especially if a couple helps each other out. If it is usually the husband's job to prepare the children's breakfast, perhaps his wife could do it one day a week while he takes over her usual task of cooking the main meal. There are no laws here, just wisdom. Jesus said, "The Sabbath was made for man, not man for the Sabbath" (Mark 2:27).

2. *Remembrance.* Remembrance is the emphasis of the sabbath command as it appears in Deuteronomy, where the Ten Commandments are listed a second time:

> Observe the Sabbath day by keeping it holy, as the LORD your God commanded you. . . . Remember that you were slaves in Egypt and that the LORD your God brought you out of there with a mighty hand and an outstretched arm. Therefore the LORD your God has commanded you

to observe the Sabbath day. (Deuteronomy 5:12, 15)

The people of Israel were to use the sabbath to remember God and his deliverance of them from slavery in Egypt. It was a weekly reminder to them that this world and its preoccupations were not ultimately what mattered. They were to look up and refocus on God, their Creator and Redeemer.

When British politician Michael Portillo announced his intention to retire from Parliament, he said,

> I don't think I will merit more than a footnote in the history of the Conservative Party. But along the way I discovered that life and career are not the same thing. Many people are miserable until they find that out.[19]

That is an important lesson to learn. Many people are far too absorbed in their work. They will almost certainly come to regret that. No one has been heard to say on their deathbed, "I wish I'd spent more time at the office." We diminish our humanity if we allow ourselves to be consumed by our job. We are not designed just to work. A regular day of rest is an important reminder of that fact. It gives us a chance to refocus on our relationship with God, which should be at the center of our lives.

Henri Blocher points out that the seventh day

> relativises the works of mankind, the contents of the six working days. It protects mankind from total absorption by the task of subduing the earth, it anticipates the dis-

tortion which makes work the sum and purpose of human life, and it informs mankind that he will not fulfill his humanity in his relation to the world which he is transforming but only when he raises his eyes above, in the blessed, holy hour of communion with the Creator. With this meaning it would be no exaggeration to state that the Sabbath sums up the difference between the Biblical and the Marxist versions. The essence of mankind is not work![20]

We might add that humankind's essence is not work but worship. Our relationship with God must come first.

We should regularly ask ourselves if work is a sphere of our service of God, as it should be, or if we have allowed it to become a rival to him. Work too often becomes an alternative god, so that our great goal is no longer to please him but rather to please the boss, achieve a target or gain promotion. It is important that we make time each day consciously to draw near to God. Our prayer should include our work offered as a service to God. Then, on one day of the week, we should give extra time to focussing on our Maker as we lay aside our normal work.

Our day of rest should never be escapism. We are not to see church as a spiritual bubble, where we can switch off from the world outside. We should rather recognize that all of life is to be lived with God and for God. We are to remind each other of that fact when we meet with other Christians and encourage each other to live in the light of it when we disperse. When we return to the world of work we should still be thinking, *How can I serve God here?*

3. *Rescue.* The sabbath points us forward to the completion of God's rescue. Adam and Eve shared God's seventh day in the Garden of Eden, but when they sinned they forfeited that "rest." Although echoes of God's perfect intentions for his creation remain, the world is spoiled. But God longs to restore it. He is determined to bring everything back to its original perfection in the seventh day. His rescue plan has been achieved by Christ through his death and resurrection, and will be consummated when he returns to earth. Then, at last, God's people will enter his "Sabbath-rest" (Hebrews 4:8-11). On that great day, all God's original plans for his creation will be fulfilled.

"Creation work" and "new creation work." Christians live in tension while we wait for Christ's return. We live in this present world and have God-given responsibilities within it: "creation work." God made the world and cares for it. He has commanded us to "fill the earth and subdue it," to work the land and "take care of it" (Genesis 1:28; 2:15). We are serving him when we obey this command. Our labor as parents, citizens, politicians and employees is not "secular work" but Christian work. We serve Christ as we serve his creation.

But Christians must not only focus on this world. We are citizens of heaven. We enjoy God's rest partially already and look forward to its fulfillment in the world to come, the new creation. With that great future in mind, Christ has given us "new creation work" to do. We are to "go and make disciples of all nations" (Matthew 28:19), proclaiming that Jesus is Lord and Savior, and calling on people to repent and believe in him.

Some, because of their particular gifts, are set apart by the church to devote themselves to the work of evangelism and pastoral ministry. There is an urgent need for many more such laborers in God's harvest field. It is the responsibility of other believers to give generously and thus provide for their financial needs (Luke 10:7; 1 Corinthians 9:4-12). But that is not the only way in which most of us should contribute to new creation work. As we live godly lives in this present world, we should pray that God would use us all as his witnesses to point people to the next world and to the Lord Jesus Christ, who can take them there. With our lives and lips we should proclaim that this world is not all there is. There is a better place, unspoiled by human sin. God, Father, Son and Holy Spirit, will be at the center, with everything and everyone finding their place and meaning in him. Then, at last, "the times will have reached their fulfillment," and God's eternal plan will be realized: "to bring all things in heaven and on earth together under one head, even Christ" (Ephesians 1:10).

● Bible Study: Colossians 3:18—4:1

Read through the whole passage and look for any repeated words and phrases. What are their implications for our understanding of "Christian service"?

Serving Christ in Our Marriages (3:18-19)

What might it mean in practice for wives to "submit"?

Are there limits?

What might it mean in practice for husbands to "love" (see Ephesians 5:25-28)?

What difference might it make if we do this "in the Lord" (v. 18)?

Serving Christ in Our Families (3:20-21)

Is obedience to our parents (Exodus 20:12) expected throughout life?

Is it possible to honor our parents without obeying them?

Where is the greatest challenge for us as Christian sons, daughters or parents?

Serving Christ in Our Jobs (3:22—4:1)

What principles can we apply today?

How do they differ from the way most people think?

What changes do they demand in our

- attitude to work?
- behavior at work?

FURTHER READING

Chapter 1: The Divine Creator

Birkett, Kirsten. *The Essence of Darwinism*. Kingsford, Australia: Matthias Media, 2001, pp. 133-42.

Blocher, Henri. *In the Beginning*. Downers Grove, Ill.: InterVarsity Press, 1984, pp. 20-24, 213-31.

Grudem, Wayne. *Systematic Theology*. Leicester, England: Inter-Varsity Press, 1994, pp. 273-309.

Johnson, Phillip. *Darwin on Trial*. Downers Grove, Ill.: InterVarsity Press, 1994.

Chapter 2: God's Design for Humanity

Wyatt, John. *Matters of Life and Death: Today's Healthcare Dilemmas in the Light of the Christian Faith*. Leicester, England: Inter-Varsity Press, 1998.

Chapter 3: God's Design for the Earth

Elsdon, Ron. *Green House Theology*. Tunbridge Wells, England: Monarch, 1992.

Stott, John. *New Issues Facing Christians Today*. London: BCA, 1999, pp. 123-42.

Wright, Christopher J. H. *Old Testament Ethics for the People of God*. Downers Grove, Ill.: InterVarsity Press, 2004, pp. 103-45.

Chapter 4: God's Design for Sex and Marriage

Ash, Christopher. *Marriage: Sex in the Service of God.* Leicester, England: Inter-Varsity Press, 2003.

Brewer, David Instone. *Divorce and Remarriage in the Bible.* Grand Rapids, Mich.: Eerdmans, 2002.

Cornes, Andrew. *Divorce and Remarriage.* London: Hodder & Stoughton, 1993.

Hsu, Al. *Singles at the Crossroads.* Downers Grove, Ill.: InterVarsity Press, 1997.

Jensen, Phillip, and Tony Payne. *Pure Sex.* Kingsford, Australia: Matthias Media, 2003.

Schmidt, Thomas E. *Straight and Narrow?* Downers Grove, Ill.: InterVarsity Press, 1995.

Stott, John. *New Issues Facing Christians Today.* London: BCA, 1999, pp. 319-44, 382-418.

Chapter 5: God's Design for Work

Carson, D. A., ed. *From Sabbath to Lord's Day.* Eugene, Ore.: Wipf and Stock, 1999.

Greene, Mark. *Thank God It's Monday.* Bletchley, England: Scripture Union, 1994.

Guinness, Os. *The Call.* Carlisle, England: Paternoster, 2001.

Pipa, Joseph. *The Lord's Day.* Fearn, England: Christian Focus, 1997.

Ryken, Leland. *Work and Leisure in Christian Perspective.* Eugene, Ore.: Wipf and Stock, 2002.

Stott, John. *New Issues Facing Christians Today.* London: BCA, 1999, pp. 185-209.

NOTES

Introduction

[1] John R. W. Stott, *New Issues Facing Christians Today* (London: BCA, 1999), pp. 39-41. Stott refers to "consummation" rather than "new creation."

[2] Vaughan Roberts, *God's Big Picture* (Leicester, England: Inter-Varsity Press, 2003), and *Life's Big Questions* (Downers Grove, Ill.: InterVarsity Press, 2004).

[3] Gordon Wenham, *Genesis 1-15* (Waco, Tex.: Word, 1987), p. 40.

Chapter One: The Divine Creator

[1] Carl Sagan, quoted in Michael Green, *Critical Choices* (Leicester, England: Inter-Varsity Press, 1995), p. 9.

[2] Douglas Coupland, *Generation X* (London: Abacas, 1996), p. 12.

[3] John Blanchard, *Does God Believe in Atheists?* (Darlington, England: Evangelical Press, 2000), p. 246.

[4] The word *accidentalism* was coined by Phillip Jensen, Anglican dean of Sydney, Australia.

[5] Richard Dawkins, *The Blind Watchmaker* (London: Penguin, 1986), p. 5.

[6] Steven Gaukroger, *It Makes Sense* (London: Scripture Union, 1996), p. 13.

[7] Douglas Adams, quoted in Blanchard, *Does God Believe in Atheists?* p. 247.

[8] Henri Blocher, *In the Beginning* (Downers Grove, Ill.: InterVarsity Press, 1984), p. 225.

[9] Charles Darwin, quoted in ibid.

[10]Charles Swinburne, *Hymn of Man,* in *Concise Oxford Dictionary of Quotations* (Oxford: Oxford University Press, 1964), p. 224.

[11]Bertrand Russell, *A Free Man's Worship,* as quoted by J. W. N. Sullivan, *Limitations of Science* (London: Pelican, 1978), p. 175.

[12]Francis Bacon, quoted in Green, *Critical Choices,* p. 29.

[13]Samuel Beckett, *Waiting for Godot,* quoted in David Watson, *Is Anyone There?* (London: Hodder & Stoughton, 1998), p. 16.

[14]Jean-Paul Sartre, *Existentialism and Humanism,* a lecture delivered in Paris in 1944, quoted in Ravi Zacharias, *A Shattered Visage* (London: Baker, 1993), p. 126.

[15]Bryan Appleyard, review of Glover, *Humanity,* in *The Sunday Times,* December 1999.

[16]Blanchard, *Does God Believe in Atheists?* p. 172.

Chapter Two: God's Design for Humanity

[1]Peter Lewis, in *Chosen for Good,* ed. Robert Horn (Eastbourne, England: Kingsway, 1986), p. 17.

[2]Francis Schaeffer, *Pollution and the Death of Man* (London: Hodder & Stoughton, 1970), p. 9.

[3]Edmund Leach, Reith Lecture (1967), quoted in George Carey, *I Believe in Man* (London: Hodder & Stoughton, 1977), p. 33.

[4]*Chicago Maroon,* November 21, 2003.

[5]Simone de Beauvoir, *The Second Sex* (London: Vintage, 1997), p. 295.

[6]Peter Singer, *Animal Liberation,* 2nd ed. (London: Pimlico Books, 1995), p. 6.

[7]"All Animals Are Equal" is the title of the first chapter of *Animal Liberation.*

[8]Peter Singer, *Practical Ethics* (Cambridge: Cambridge University Press, 1993), p. 87.

[9]Helga Kuhse and Peter Singer, *Should the Baby Live?* (Oxford: Oxford University Press, 1985), pp. 155-61.

[10]Francis Crick, quoted in John Blanchard, *Does God Believe in Atheists?* (Darlington, England: Evangelical Press, 2000), p. 16.

[11]Richard Dawkins, *The Selfish Gene* (Oxford: Oxford University Press, 1989), p. ix.

[12]Donald MacKay, *The Clockwork Image* (Leicester, England: Inter-Varsity Press, 1974), pp. 40-45.

[13]These points are based on those in a talk by John Stott at the London Institute for Contempory Christianity (July 1985).

[14]John Calvin *Institutes of the Christian Religion* 1.3.3.

[15]Schaeffer, *Pollution and the Death of Man*, pp. 36-37.

[16]Amrit Dhillon, *The Times*, June 22, 2004.

[17]Ellie Lee, "The Moral Maze," *Radio 4*, July 6, 2004.

[10]See Vaughan Roberts, *Life's Big Questions* (Downers Grove, Ill.: InterVarsity Press, 2003), pp. 49-58.

Chapter Three: God's Design for the Earth

[1]Joanna Macy, quoted in Roger S Gottlieb, ed., *This Sacred Earth* (London: Routledge, 1996), p. 3.

[2]Data on the Antarctic ozone hole taken from the U.S. Environmental Protection Agency <www.epa.gov/ozone/science/hole/size.html>.

[3]See J. E. Lovelock, *Gaia: A New Look at Life on Earth* (New York: Oxford University Press, 1979), and later publications.

[4]C. S. Lewis, *The Problem of Pain* (London: Bles, 1940).

[5]Gordon J. Wenham, *Genesis 1-15* (Waco, Tex.: Word, 1987), p. 39.

[6]Christopher J. H. Wright, *Old Testament Ethics for the People of God* (Downers Grove, Ill.: InterVarsity Press, 2004), p. 131.

[7]Tim Chester, *Good News to the Poor* (Leicester, England: Inter-Varsity Press, 2004), p. 25.

[8]Ian McHarg, *Design with Nature* (New York: Doubleday, 1969), p. 26.

[9]Wright, *Old Testament Ethics*, p. 121.

[10]John Stott, *New Issues Facing Christians Today* (London: BCA, 1999), p. 135.

[11]Wright, *Old Testament Ethics*, p. 131.

[12]Stott, *New Issues Facing Christians Today*, p. 135.

[13]Ranald Macaulay, *The Great Commissions in Christianity in a Changing World*, ed. Michael Schluter (London: Marshal Pickering, 2000), p. 41.

Chapter Four: God's Design for Sex and Marriage

[1]Mike Starkey, *God, Sex and Generation X* (London: SPCK, 1997), p. 47.

[2]National survey of sexual attitudes and lifestyles, 2001.

[3]Glenn Stanton, "Fact Sheet on Divorce in America" <www.smartmarriages.com /divorce_brief.html>: "In 1970, 3% of all people over 18 years of age were divorced. In 1994, that number had climbed to 9%."

[4]Christopher Ash, *Marriage* (Leicester, England: Inter-Varsity Press, 2003), p. 39.

[5]Patrick F. Fagan and Robert E. Rector, "The Effects of Divorce on America" <www.heritage.org/Research/Family/BG1373.cfm>.

[6]John Richardson, *God, Sex and Marriage* (London: St. Matthias Press, 1998), p. 19.

[7]Thomas E Schmidt, *Straight and Narrow?* (Downers Grove, Ill.: InterVarsity Press, 1995), p. 44.

[8]Ibid., p. 45.

[9]John Gray, *Men Are from Mars, Women Are from Venus* (New York: Harper-Collins, 1992).

[10]Christopher Ash, *Marriage: Sex in the Service of God* (Leicester, England: Inter-Varsity Press, 2003).

[11]Sources cited in ibid., p. 128.

[12]Ibid., p. 120.

[13]Ibid., p. 131.

[14]Ibid., p. 126.

[15]Premier Radio Survey 2003.

[16]C. S. Lewis, *The Four Loves* (London: Fount, 1977), p. 87.

[17]*Cosmopolitan*, September 2003.

[18]Ian Stewart Gregory, *No Sex Please, We're Single* (Eastbourne, England: Kingsway, 1997), p. 133.

[19]Schmidt, *Straight and Narrow?* p. 47.

[20]Richard Kirker, quoted in Brian Edwards, ed., *Homosexuality: The Straight Agenda* (Leominster, England: Day One, 1998), p. 184.

[21]James C. Dobson, *Straight Talk* (London: Hodder & Stoughton, 1992), p. 51.

[22]Ash, *Marriage*, p. 40.

[23]See "Further Reading" section on p. 119.

[24]Church of England, *Marriage* (London: Church House Publishing, 2000), p. 15.

Chapter Five: God's Design for Work

[1]Doug Sherman and William Hendricks, *Your Work Matters to God* (Colorado Springs: NavPress, 1987), p. 16.

[2]Ibid., p. 7.

[3]Abraham Kuyper, quoted in Os Guinness, *The Call* (Carlisle, England: Paternoster, 2001), p. 35.

[4]Leland Ryken, *Work and Leisure in Christian Perspective* (Eugene, Ore.: Wipf and Stock, 2002), p. 65.

[5]Guinness, *Call*, p. 32.

[6]Mark Greene, *Thank God It's Monday,* 3rd ed. (Bletchley, England: Scripture Union, 2001), p. 30.

[7]Sherman and Hendricks, *Your Work Matters to God*, p. 82.

[8]Martin Luther, sermon of 1525, quoted in Gene Edward Veith, *God at Work* (Wheaton, Ill.: Crossway, 2002), p. 65.

[9]John Stott, *New Issues Facing Christians Today* (London: BCA, 1999), p. 194.

[10]Greene, *Thank God It's Monday*, p. 18.

[11]Ryken, *Work and Leisure in Christian Perspective*, p. 148.

[12]Martin Luther, sermon on Matthew 6:24-34, quoted in ibid., p. 135.

[13]Martin Luther, lecture on Genesis 31:3, quoted in Stott, *New Issues Facing Christians Today*, p. 193.

[14]Stott, *New Issues Facing Christians Today*, p. 195.

[15]Gordon MacDonald, *When Men Think Private Thoughts* (Nashville: Thomas Nelson, 1996), pp. 4, 5.

[16]Peter Cohan, *The Gospel According to the Harvard Business School* (London: Penguin, 1981).

[17]Mark Greene, *Supporting Christians at Work: Administry How-to Guide 2,* no. 6.

[18]See the "Further Reading" section on page 126 for books that outline the different positions.

[19]Michael Portillo, quoted in *The Times,* February 22, 2004.

[20]Henri Blocher, *In The Beginning* (Downers Grove, Ill.: InterVarsity Press, 1984), p. 57.